MEETINGS
MAYHEM!

**A humorous but factual look at the
serious business of making meetings happen**

All stories compiled by
Terry Matthews-Lombardo, CMP

Advance Praise for Meetings Mayhem!

For some of us, we have spent our entire careers in events and meetings. And no matter what happened the last time around, we always start fresh on the next event and plan for each program to be perfect, flawless, and achieved with impeccable execution. Further, we design and create our events to be **so** outstanding and unforgettable that they will be **the** experience that our clients and guests remember and talk about **forever**. In our heads, our professional meetings will be **the industry standard** for education.

But instead, a week out there is a major fire at the venue, or the restaurant you have specifically chosen as 'the perfect location' unexpectedly shuts down. Or the Mayor's seated dinner for sixty VIPs just had forty more delegates added two hours before the meal was plated.

Or, we have a pandemic, and everything on the planet just stops.

I invite you to enjoy this wonderful book and find out how these amazing professionals handle their meetings and events flawlessly. See how they correct an impossible situation with grace and ease as they act as tremendous taskmasters while their clients and guests never know what was happening behind the scenes.

—Colleen A. Rickenbacher, CMP, CSEP, CPC, CPECP
Global Protocol, Etiquette & Civility Academy
www.globalpecacademy.com
Professional Speaker and Author of multiple books on industry standards and global accepted practices

From the Voice of the Industry:

"I have known TML since her early days in the meeting/event business. Over more years that either of us would admit, we have interacted as professional colleagues, volunteers in industry organizations and, always as friends. Now, as I grudgingly approach retirement, I can say that throughout those years her positive energy and professionalism is what motivated me to maintain our friendship. For some time, I have been aware of Terry's writing skills as she began to reveal that additional talent first in her blogs in the Orlando Sentinel and now on her own industry focused travel blog. The natural evolution was for her to next write a book, and she has. It is a wonderful, easy to read compilation of fun, entertaining and educational tales of the challenging professional (and not so professional) experiences that she and many others have managed to power through and still live to laugh about. And it arrives at a time when we all crave something to make us smile. This book will surely do it for readers whether you are in this industry or just looking at it from another viewpoint. It's a joy to read a good story, and this book is full of them."

—Rod Abraham, the Rod Abraham Group
Meetings & Events Industry Strategic Consultant
Advisor to Small Business Entrepreneurs
http://www.rodabrahamgroup.com/
https://www.linkedin.com/in/rod-abraham-982b494/

*To meeting and event planners everywhere
who love their jobs even when things
go horribly. . . terribly. . . wrong.*

THANK YOU!

With generous thanks to both Tracey and Carolyn, you know who you are, for all the proofreading, corrections, and most of all the enlightening conversations (with and without adult beverages) that took place in order to get this book organized.

PLEASE NOTE:

All stories and details contained in this book are true. However, in some cases, names and locations have been changed or avoided altogether to prevent pissing off certain folks and entities in addition to potentially giving lawyers some extra business. Also, because of the ever-changing dynamics of the internet and personal contacts, any web addresses, links, or other contact information provided within this book may have changed since publication so, just as your mother always warned you, exercise caution when surfing the worldwide web. (Well, she did tell you that, didn't she?)

TABLE OF CONTENTS

PREFACE

If you have been in the meetings and events industry for any length of time, you know that on good days even the most organized conclaves still have their challenging moments. And on bad days, those encounters can quickly turn into a calamity.

calamity: a disastrous situation or event
disastrous: a calamitous event, having potentially seriously damaging results

At those crucial moments when the tide is turning from earlier in the day when the boss said to you, "Great job with this program's kickoff!" to ten minutes later when you hear, "What do you mean we can't get the power back on RIGHT NOW in this ballroom!", the question that all planners face is how to react. Do you:

A. Visibly panic via hyperventilation, exaggerated eye roll-ing, and excessive jazz hands, then run and hide, hoping that the problem will be over when they find you?
B. Cooley laugh it off saying, "No big deal, I've got this!", then turn around and inwardly scream while trying to figure out what to do?

1

C. Immediately get on your cell phone and pretend you're calling for someone that can fix the problem so you look like a strong leader when in reality you just cannot even focus on who to call at this horrible, potentially disastrous moment in time?

D. Breathe, smile, and try to calmly deal with the situation at hand?

Depending on the size and scope of the crises du jour, most planners have done all of the above and have lived to talk about it which is how we acquired all the stories contained in this book. More importantly, for the most part, these planners have kept their jobs despite the outcome of the predicament at hand. Mostly because in the end, as they say on Broadway, "the show must go on!" It may have crossed the finished line in a different format or venue from the one that was originally planned, but somehow the production reaches that home stretch. My hope to anyone reading this book is that you will find it both educational and humorous, but most of all very entertaining.

It is important to note that each of the following stories are absolutely true. Ask any of our planners if these shocking things really happened and they will automatically respond, "We can't make this stuff up, people!"

No truer words were ever spoken.

CHAPTER ONE

Did My Speaker Just Sucker Punch the AV Guy?

As told to tml by Saira Banu Kianes, CMP, HMCC

When meeting planning gets hot. . .
Well, my first husband always told me, "you attract trouble," and maybe, possibly he was correct in this instance.

You see, early in my career I was the lead planner in charge of a partner's meeting in which I hired many high-level professional speakers to present and motivate the attendees throughout the multi day conference. As any planner knows, the handling of speakers can require coordinating a lot of details while providing white glove customer service, but I felt totally confident of my abilities, that is until the end of day one which was before any of the VIPs or speakers had even arrived on site. Or so I thought.

You see, a couple of us gathered in the hotel bar that evening to review things and relax together. At some point a rather attractive and debonair British gentleman sat down next to me expressing an interest in joining "the fun" it appeared we were having. This was uncomfortable to me for several reasons not the least of which was that we were all out in a professional, working capacity, plus I was newly divorced and still a little uncertain about having a guy paying attention to me which he most definitely was. Especially while at a bar.

And my awkwardness was showing during the brief conversation with this man during which I must have indicated that I was, indeed, *working* that evening. I then discovered that he had an entirely different idea of exactly *what type of work* I was referring to when one of the AV guys on our team that knew my personal situation came to my defense and strongly expressed his verbal protection of me. This quickly lit an unwanted fuse with our British "gentleman" who wasted no time in replying with his fist. I watched in shock as he swiftly delivered a sucker punch directly into the face of my AV guy-turned-guardian angel.

"You said you were *working*!" The Brit shouted at me while trying to defend his uncontrollable temper in the resulting chaos.

Oh boy.

After securing an ice pack for my friend's face, I quickly excused myself from any further embarrassment at the bar and attempted to return to my room only to be followed and pestered while in route by, you guessed it, the obnoxious Brit with a solid left hook. The nerve of him! Being an adult, albeit a little shaken up by this humiliating and unfortunate turn of events, I did manage to maintain my professional dignity and dissuade any further evening nonsense while sending him on his way.

But then came the morning, and guess who shows up in our VIP green room to get ready for his rehearsal as our featured headlining keynote speaker? You guessed it! Imagine my horror when I discovered that Mr.-one-and-only was the world-famous broadcaster hired (for major money, by the way) to jump start this conference's opening session! Needless to say, he offered no apology and in fact seemed quite pleased that his temporary "I'm calling the shots now, lady" status now put him firmly in a control position.

To my credit, I somehow stuck with my no-nonsense work mode, although I'm confident I was showing ten shades of red every time that man even glanced at me. He, being the pompous human being that he was, maintained an aloof level of involvement whenever he was in my vicinity, which considering I was charged with top level customer care for all our speakers, was happening quite often that morning.

And if tensions weren't bad enough between us, as a topper to further taunt me at one point and to solidify his arrogance, he requested that I make a spa appointment for his wife that he casually mentioned had accompanied him to the conference. *Ewww.*

Lessons learned? You bet, and they include:

- ✓ Always review photographs, preferably head shots, of your VIPs and speakers. Share those with everyone on your management team to avoid, well, refer back to my painful story above and remember how this played out. Had I any inkling of what he looked like, that whole raucous bar scene might have been avoided.
- ✓ Always stay professional while you are on site working your program. This includes even when you relax a little with your team as you never know who you will meet up with and when that will happen because as we all know, first impressions do count!

NOTES: Saira's BIO can be found at the end of her next story, Incentive "Perks." And, trust me, you won't want to miss her story about that memorable *"special event!"*

CHAPTER TWO

Incentive "Perks"

As told to tml by Saira Banu Kianes, CMP, HMCC

Most **incentive*** trips are remembered for their awesome destinations, magnificent upscale resort hotels and the never-ending number of activities combined with unique food and beverage events that are all packaged together for a five-star attendee experience. But for those participating in meeting planner Saira Banu Kianes's corporate program held at a fabulous resort in Cabo San Lucas, Mexico, well, something else may come to mind when they reflect on that great trip. It was an event that took place on the last day of the program and proved to be quite embarrassing not to mention painful for one person in particular. Here is what happened...

Our final day's activity involved taking about twenty people, roughly ten qualifiers and their guests, out on a catamaran that allowed everyone to swim, dive, and snorkel at a few stops throughout the morning. It is a pretty standard activity for a beach resort, and the only thing that made this a bit unusual was that one guest was wearing a speedo bathing suit that, oh gosh. Let's just say it left nothing to the imagination! There was absolutely no support in this man's nether-region, and to be frank, this guy was particularly well endowed. He was also rather enjoying his notoriety to the point that he was a bit flirtatious with more than just his own partner. As the group's planner and escort, it was my job to make sure that everyone was comfortable and having a great time, so I was doing my levelheaded best (not easy on a rocking ship!) to avoid any awkward scenes, although in my wildest dreams I could never have predicted the "rough waters" ahead.

Since the morning had been highly active and full of all those water sports, on the way back to the resort everyone kind of settled into a calm, rather lazy mode as most people were just enjoying the sunshine along with the on-board refreshments or simply watching the boat sprint through the choppy waves in quiet contemplation.

Meanwhile, the "speedo-man", apparently exhausted, was sleeping–face up–on the buoyant, webbed portion connecting the two hulls of the catamaran which is a common practice on these ships. At one point his companion lying next to him must have mentioned the need for a sunscreen application to his back side. Next thing I know I'm hearing a ghastly *"errrma-god!"* followed by a loud wailing of *"holymotherofmercy!"* coming from the happy couple now causing quite a bit of ruckus and attention on our small watercraft. In one of those shocking *this-didn't-really-just-happen* moments, apparently while spee-do-man was rolling over to accept that anticipated slather of sunscreen, our ship also lurched up with a swell and slammed back down causing his, um, err, ah, "extra-large-now-extended *thingee*" to get caught in one of the rope coils that was holding that web frame taught. Oh. My.

(Yes, now that I'm looking at that last sentence, I am kind of in disbelief myself. But you just cannot make this stuff up, folks!)

To this day I could still not tell you the exact wording of what transpired in the next frenzied conversations but let me just say that the Captain had to stop the boat in order to attend to the situation at hand. That man's "*willy*" was indeed *stuck real good* between some rope coils! And being that it was a fairly small, intimate boat, there was no way to hide this from the other passengers. But somehow the Captain managed to steer us back into port where everyone quickly disembarked, except of course, for the man and his partner, both of whom were beyond humiliation and one of which was simply stuck face down not able to move and writhing in pain. To his credit, once in port the Captain was quickly able to cut the coils freeing "the prisoner", and medics from on shore had already been called to supply ice packs and pain killers.

In the end, I'm sure the amount of tequila he consumed that night was more than sufficient to replace the pain killers, and gratefully that was done in the privacy of his hotel suite as that couple was a no show to our final night farewell dinner which was fine by me.

But wait, there's more! He did show up during breakfast the next morning right before the group airport departure, and as you can imagine, everyone's eyes naturally kept going to "that special place" on his body that would forever be remembered as, well, a particular *perk* of that incentive trip! Being a reactive planner always wanting to quickly correct uncomfortable guest situations, I then took a leap of faith that we all needed to turn this uncomfortable situation into something we might be able to laugh about later. Hastily, I took one of the waiter's white aprons and using my black felt marker made a large arrow pointing upward and wrote, "Hey-my eyes are up here," and then ceremoniously hung it around his neck. To my relief, both he and his partner–along with everyone else-finally got a good belly laugh out in the open about that whole unforeseeable and equally unbelievable ordeal that would forever mark this incentive program as one for the record books!

*an incentive** is an award of some kind, either a gift or trip, given by companies to "incentivize" employees to a higher level of performance. In this context, the incentive was an entire trip to Cabo San Lucas including the travel costs, hotel accommodations, all food and beverages consumed during the trip and other amenities enjoyed such as the daily activities.

Lessons Learned:

- ✓ Not sure there is really anything here to learn except to expect the unexpected (?!)
- ✓ Accept that some situations are just going to leave you speechless. This was *definitely* one of those!

SAIRA BANU KIANES BIO: Saira was born in India but moved to the USA as a child bride after an arranged marriage. As a bi-lingual new American, she quickly became a travel counselor and a young entrepreneur while learning her craft in the meetings industry. Now a veteran meeting professional with a specialty in servicing medical, pharmaceutical and IT companies, she manages both meetings and incentive programs all over the globe in such intriguing locations as Dubai, Seoul, Slovenia, Malta, and Croatia just to name a few. When not traveling you can usually find her working in the garden where she grows vegetables and spices that can be found in her well-used kitchen that always smells of exotic dishes. Saira is also an avid seamstress and to date has made over 2000 safety masks during the pandemic, all of which were donated to appreciative front line workers in her New Jersey community.

www.banueventsolutions.com

CHAPTER THREE

Fun with Food Trucks?

By Carolyn Browning, CMP, CMM, HMCC

My colleague and I were working with a long-term client planning their **consumer goods conference*** in California. During this annual conference they would showcase products and services from some of their own clients with two goals: getting additional investors for their new product development, and to add some elements of fun.

One year at the closing reception they wanted to have some local food vendors participate so we set out to get a food truck from a local burger place. No biggie, right? Food trucks continue to be all the rage, and in my planner's mind, I figured this shouldn't be much different than bringing in another outside vendor, maybe just adding a permit or two. Easy-peasy (ish!).

Until it's not!

Even before the complicated discovery process began for the necessary permits, I started my planner's checklist of what it would take from A-Z to make this happen. Where? When? What are the costs? All these things and more started appearing on my very neat, tidy, and organized chart because as planners we just love to check details off the list.

First up was the easiest piece of the puzzle–confirming that the hotel would allow the food truck. Since they had let us bring in outside food for other functions we had held there in past years, they agreed and reminded me of the COI (certificate of insurance) needed from the vendor as well as the requirement to pay what is called an "outside catering fee" to the hotel since they would be "giving up" potential food revenue to the actual food truck vendor. And yes, this is in addition to what we would be paying to the food truck for the actual food, so cha-ching!

Next, due the size of the truck–I had discovered it would need 70' of parking space and 14' overhead clearance (!?!) -we learned that we could not park it in front of the hotel, nor would it fit in the driveway. My hotel CSM (convention service manager, aka a meeting planner's best friend) suggested a location behind the property. After further discussion and a walk through of this area we realized that meant our attendees would need to take the elevator down one floor and then walk out the back door just to get those yummy burgers, but shrug-shrug, okay. Let them work up an appetite along that journey. And the client finally agreed, so that was that. Tick another box off my ever-growing checklist.

Now, because I know you're on the edge of your seats here, back to those pesky permits. I was first instructed to contact the city in order to obtain one for street parking, and as a point of reference, I started this process in late March for a conference to be held mid-May, a solid three months forward. With the help of Mr. Google, I began searching on the city's website for parking permit information. After clicking around a lot (shocking, a government website that was not very intuitive or helpful!) I finally found information on temporary parking permits. But that just started the beginning of the process with my first email sent on Friday, March 29 which was promptly greeted with an auto-response that the office was closed and would reopen on Monday. Okay then, no problem, so, I called back on Monday (remembering to factor in the time difference between my office on East Coast and theirs on the West) only to be greeted with that series of dreaded prompts that takes you into never-never land, and sometimes (who am I kidding–all the time) leaves you scratching your head. Okie-dokey. Once I figured out what series of buttons to push, I was promptly put on hold. For 15 minutes. With no voicemail option.

Patience, Carolyn.

I switched gears and put my thinking cap on to come up with a new game plan to expedite this process. Let's see if the hotel CSM had a contact downtown and yes, she did! Remember when I mentioned the CSM can be a planner's BFF? Score! Called a different number, this time at the Business License Department and got an actual person (!). Was told I would be emailed an out-of-city business application. Oh, and I would also need to call another department to get a temporary parking permit. Hmmm. Seems I was already seeing a pattern here–voicemail jail, being shuffled around to multiple departments before finally being told differing pieces of information. Then what?

Fast forward – got paperwork I needed from the food truck (their business license certificate) along with updated and more specific details on the truck size and the requisite clearance restrictions needed to park that baby. But would you believe it took until the beginning of May to get all the final paperwork together on my end? Of course you would! And remember, the conference started on May 14.

In the end, I finally got through to someone at City Hall who was very helpful. That is until she got to the point in the conversation where she said, "You must submit the final paperwork and pick up the permit and the required 'no parking' signs in person." Um, all righty? But then I learned the permitting office is closed on Fridays and, you guessed it, I wasn't arriving until Friday. Lucky for us we were able to enlist help from some of the client's local staff who was able to rush over and pick up the permit and required signage.

But you just know it's not going to end here, right?

We then learned that the previously approved hotel space was actually considered a "no parking/red zone" because it was next to the hotel loading dock making it a no-go for our food truck. Okay then! We were then reassigned a space across the street, and you would think no biggie, right? But let's take an imaginary walk together as we stroll the path from where my guests were coming from, the hotel convention area, and get them to the food truck, now located across the street. We discovered the most direct path was (surprise!) to walk them through the less-than-attractive hotel parking garage, and let's just say the client was not exactly on board with this option. At all! And I certainly couldn't blame them as I wasn't either.

We regrouped yet again and found a better solution by using a combination of our staff along with hotel employees to guide guests to the elevators and then walk them across the street to our truck. Wow, what a process!

So, and this is where it gets even better, the day of event comes, and my colleague goes to check the six parking spots where we had already placed our city issued and approved no parking signs earlier in the day. Um, did I mention that this location was near the beach? And that car owners had a 'beach-mentality parking' meaning, signs? What signs? Yeah, there was that. Luckily our no parking zone enforcement signs were posted as beginning at 4pm, and all but one car was moved in time. And that last car? Well, after having several polite and persuasive words with this surfer dude, he finally moved his vehicle.

Great. We. Are. Ready! Except we're not.

The truck comes and darn it was huge! They look at the assigned parking spot and advise us they cannot park there. *Say what?*

"Sorry. It's on a slope and we can't park on a slope. That's not good for food prep."

"Um, okay?"

Back to Plan A, or was it B, C? Who even knew at this point? Plus, that time clock was ticking away to the moment when our attendees would be stepping up and placing an order! In the end, the hotel let us go back to the area by their loading dock as it was after normal operating hours and our truck was not really blocking anything.

By now I was beside myself worried about that precious permit issued for a totally different location and being the rule-follower I am, I called the number on said permit to get "readjusted" permission. BIG MISTAKE! Imagine my surprise in discovering that number was for the police since (another surprise!) they needed to inspect/approve the "no parking" signs' locations and would have helped move/tow any cars that had not yet moved for us. Wow. Just wow.

The genuinely nice police sergeant told me we did not have permission to park there due to it being a "red zone." After some back and forth on this getting-hotter-by-the-minute topic, what it boiled down to was that IF they happened to drive by to inspect, the truck could get ticketed and towed. Yep. Exact words. And you can imagine, at this point **there was no freakin' way I would allow them to tow this thing!**

NOTE TO SELF: Veteran planner learns valuable lesson about keeping her mouth shut!

So, how did it end?

Guests loved it? *Check.* Client provided something different and fun? *Check. Check.* Any cops show up? *Negative.*

Score one for this weary planner!

*__consumer goods conference:__ Highlighting companies that sell products to consumers

Lessons learned:

✓ Ask plenty of questions, then ask some more! Look at your event from all angles and remember that no details are too small to be taken for granted.

✓ When working with a government entity (city, town, etc.) start as early as possible and be persistent. Get as much information as you can to start the process and fill in as it moves along. I had photos of that food truck along with basic specs but in the end needed so much more to complete the task.

✓ Planners definitely need to arrive on site with enough time to thoroughly review and then revise plans as needed. Unexpected things will happen and sometimes you need a Plan B (and in my case Plan C!) in order to complete a task.

CAROLYN BROWNING BIO: Browning is a veteran Meeting Professional who has earned both her CMP as well as the CMM, and more recently added the HMCC. She works with a variety of clients through her company, MEETing Needs, LLC.

Beyond that she is a highly awarded industry Educator, Facilitator, and Connector. Plus, she's an all-out Disney fanatic, can name all the rides and Dwarfs and even admits to enjoying a Disneymoon. Oh, and if you are ever up for a Disney trivia challenge, Carolyn will always say, "game on!"

www.carolynbrowning.com

CHAPTER FOUR

Not So Entertaining!

By Suzan Bunn, CMP, CHSP, CHE

STORY OVERVIEW: In 1976, having graduated two years prior from UCF (then Florida Technological University) with an elementary education degree, I was thrown into the role of a meeting planner for a Florida based financial trade association after serving only six months as a receptionist. I barely knew what a trade association was and had zero understanding of what a meeting planner did. But that was very typical of that time in our past as that is exactly how the meeting industry started…with support staff planning meetings and events of all shapes, sizes, and budgets. In addition, there were no resources or support for the meeting planners back then. That was to come later in Orlando, when the author of this very book help charter the Central Florida Chapter of Meeting Planners International and assisted, as did many of us still active in this community, in making the meeting professional industry the vital career path that it is today.

So, here are where my stories of mayhem begin…

From my start as a meeting and event planner at that association, I was tasked with creating over thirty different business gatherings annually that ranged in size from elite twenty-member committee meetings to 50–150-person executive training seminars and culminating in over 1,000 top executives attending our annual convention. And that was just for starters! The annual convention alone was a very prestigious affair attended by our CEO, Board members and top executives, and its' purpose was to highlight the different financial institutions' accomplishments. This was done through keynote general sessions, legislative updates, topical breakouts, meal functions and sports tournaments, and then culminated with a final night gala extravaganza. The demographics of my group were mostly wealthy forty to sixty-year-old savings and loan/bank executives - think financial and technical minded men - plus their spouses. As a Florida based association we were mandated to meet in state, and at the time, there were only three five-star resorts that could comfortably handle a group of our size. My how things have changed since then!

In accomplishing my newly minted job as a meeting planner, I quickly discovered that one of my biggest challenges would come in booking the high-level speakers and entertainment to support all these events. Again, because this was in the early days of our whole industry blooming, there really were only a couple of reputable booking agencies (now referred to as speaker bureaus) for obtaining top level speakers and acceptable-to-us celebrity entertainment. Those that were out there were hard to find and awfully expensive; so, it was incumbent on me to personally research and book these important acts. Now remember, this procedure was being undertaken by a fresh out of college twenty-something who was not only new to her job but also foreign to the industry. Plus, my resources were limited.

With all that in mind, what I am sharing are some very embarrassing and really-learned-the-hard-way life lessons about my entertainment booking blunders during those early days. On the plus side as I look back now, at least it is with a laugh and a smile.

For instance, at one of my first annual conventions I booked a blast-from-the-past singing group, the Platters, who were famous in the 50's and seemed to fit my associations' demographic meaning my attendees would have grown up listening to their top hits music and would get excited to see them in person at our closing event. My "research" involved a fellow meeting planner directing me to a booking site for "oldies groups," so armed with all that knowledge (cough), I went right to work. Once I found "The Platters" and negotiated with their "spokesperson" what I felt was a fair price based on our budget, the deal was confirmed.

A triumph for me, until that fateful Saturday night of my gala.

"The Platters" did show up, and it could be said that they performed. It would also be remembered that they CRASHED. BIG time!

You see as a newbie to this industry I did not realize that during this time frame with those popular 50's groups there had been no copyrighting of performance materials or, gulp, even the group members themselves. The result was that yes, I had booked "The Platters." But what I quickly learned was that any group that had one original Platters group member, even if it were an instrumentalist or songwriter, could put together "a group" and call themselves by that famous name, in our case, "The Platters."

Yep. Turned out "my" Platters had none-as in not one! -of the original singers in it. Worse yet, no member of that group was able to carry a tune! You might even have called them "The Saucers", wonk-wonk, because that's how flat they were as performers.

Okay then, moving on!

The next big entertainment lesson I learned about in a very costly way was a creature called the contract ADDENDUM. Called "a creature" because it can grow and get ugly very quickly without your realization. It is a creature that contains the wants and needs of the speaker or entertainer above and beyond what their basic contract requirements were that both parties had already signed. Let me give you some examples of added items my past entertainment bookings requested or at least tried to slide by us, sometimes successfully.

First up is the time I booked the Fifth Dimension, an extremely popular singing group of five, or at least that is the number that showed in the contract. We soon learned (through that nasty addendum) their group of five would turn into well, I actually lost count of how many musicians and family members "had to" come along for this one-night performance. And they required accommodations for all of them. For four nights. Plus, multi day recreation options and "other expenses as needed." I will never forget the moment when that resort presented me with an itemized bill–for day one-that included food, drink, and bicycle rentals for four hours, for twenty-five people. Gulp! Apparently, that "ding" was covered under the term "recreation option" in their nasty addendum. Ouch! In my defense it was neither clearly defined as such nor was there a dollar amount attached, but from the looks of that bill I was certain we I had paid for gold plated cycles!

Next up was the female soloist–I don't want to name names but trust me it was someone on the top of billboard charts at the time–who wanted milk baths twice a day. Sounds simple, right? A little luxurious milk lotion bubble bath in a hot tub drawn by her suite butler at our five star resort.

Oh. No.

This star required a bathtub filled to her chin with **real** milk. Twice a day.

Both strange and expensive. And as a side note, also later located in that "creature addendum" under personal comforts.

And my last story involves a clause that definitely should be placed in your entertainment contract dealing with professionalism. This clause should include something about content in line with your audiences' rating standards and the performance of contracted person(s) as it relates to a client cancellation and/or a lesser fee due to the actual performance delivered. I know, a lot of wording, but let me explain.

A truly embarrassing situation which I still cannot wipe from my mind involved a well-known award-winning performer, who at the time of our booking, was riding the wave of his own wild stardom. In his mind there was not anything off limits that he should not say or do in front of a packed ballroom under the guise of "I'm a top star and everyone loves me." At some point early in his performance and to our utter shock and humiliation, this entertainer began cursing out the audio-visual tech working on the stage lighting because it was too bright for him. I'm not exaggerating when I report that he actually said over the microphone to our thousand plus audience of Executives and VIPs, "If this mother@#%!^*# AV guy doesn't get it right I'm walking off this effin' stage NOW!"

We had no recourse but to take the hit and deal with it. My only consolation was in knowing he was the one that suffered from a total loss of reputation not to mention fans that night.

My final embarrassing learn-on-the-job training tip came the year I ignored all reasoning and went rogue as I planned a 50s dance party and suggested that everyone come in costume. The fact that I could even convince my boss to let me do it still amazes me. Remember when I told you this audience was all financial and banking executives, aka "suits?" Yeah. End of story.

But not the end of lessons learned for me at that job. My takeaway from that event was that even though it appears like you're doing the same thing, providing the same type of entertainment year after year, you have to realize it's what they like and want, not your individual preference as the meeting planner.

Lessons Learned:

✓ Know your audience–go with their gut; not yours.
✓ Utilize an entertainment booking agent or a speaker bureau, who not only knows the tricks of the trade, but who can look out for you and your group.
✓ Have your legal counsel or attorney carefully review all details of your entertainment contract, to ensure all logistic details and ancillary fees, i.e., transportation, performance dates and time., etc. are accounted for and outlined therein.
✓ Pay special attention to the contract addendum, which can be more costly than the contract expenses.
✓ Know that you can negotiate and un-negotiate anything.
✓ Smile – entertainment is meant to be enjoyed by all. Even the planner!

SUZAN BUNN BIOGRAPHY: Currently an agent with Expedia Cruise Ships Center–but mostly retired-Ms. Bunn spent a combined 40 productive years with the aforementioned state trade association followed by executive positions at two Central Florida CVBs. More recently you could find her at the UCF Rosen School of Hospitality Management where she was teaching meeting and event planning as well as destination sales, marketing, and career development to the industry newbies. Despite sharing some of these eye-opening stories (plus more) from her numerous years of trying to "get it right" when it came to meeting planning, most of her students still chose this industry and actually went on to make their own mistakes and triumphs along the way, and triumphed. A lifelong advocate of the hospitality industry as well as many spiritual, scholastic, and charitable organizations, Suzan currently volunteers with United Against Poverty's STEP Program, and is Vice Chair of The Purpose Network, a non-profit. She is also a long-standing member of First Baptist of Orlando and the Orange County Toastmasters Club.

https://www.linkedin.com/in/suzanbunn

CHAPTER FIVE

Lend Me an Ear?

By Julie Wilharm Clark

During the ".com" boom, tradeshows and live events were the biggest and best. We saw small software companies grow and become public literally overnight. It was an amazing time to be in the events and experiential marketing world. It appears nothing was too expensive or usual. It was also the era where the customer was not always first, many times because corporate and management put their wants and desires at the top of the list. This led to tradeshows getting excessive - all about the expensive dinners, four-hour lunches, high-end gadget swag and the sales team working as few booth hours as possible, always with the goal of quickly moving on to those outrageously expensive evenings of client entertainment. This was not everyone or every company's culture, but at the time it was common in the technology and software fields of business. And all this is worth mentioning in this story because it sets the stage for one of the most unique and strange situations I had been faced with in my thirty-year career.

This particular show where "the incident" happened was one of the premier events that took place on the West Coast every fall, and this year the show was in October, a month that naturally lends itself–many times unintentionally-to some potentially macabre happenings. For me, this was one of those. Due to the enormous size and scope of this convention center tradeshow, it was famous for having the best exhibits, the sharpest attendees, and the most outrageous experiences, but as I would soon find out, this year would top them all.

Being the main planner and organizer for this company, it was my job to advance the show to oversee the booth set up and get everything organized for a long week of meetings, meals, product demos and any other extraordinary experiences that could be imagined. If you work in this industry you know it's always fun as you watch your ideas and dreams come to life after months of pre-planning done back in the office. Watching the electric drops laid out on the trade show floor, putting together those impressive press kits and swag bags, holding your breath as the booth graphics are installed and the tech team starts to test those all-important demo stations that will wow your customers and sell your product to them. It's all part of the excitement and build up when you're involved in these enormous trade shows. But at some point as you end those long, tedious days of set up you finally declare, perfect - so far. Whew! And that's when you move on to the final stage of preparation which is training the staff who will work the booth.

This is also the part in my story when things fell apart. In particular, "some **thing**" really did fall.

As the team leader it was my job to conduct the **pre-con meeting*** with the entire team. We start this process in the booth to acquaint them with the lay out and to physically walk through how they will greet customers and present their sales pitch. It's a combination of a logistical run through as well as a motivational meeting to get that sales force excited about the anticipated busy days ahead during the show.

So, on the eve of the trade show opening day, I conducted our in-booth training over at the convention center and then joined the team as we regrouped at the hotel for a lively happy hour in the lobby bar. After that, everyone is free to go off in their own smaller groups for dinner and I sent them away with both a goodbye and a reminder about tomorrow's call time as they slowly started to go their separate ways. For the most part, they all understand the need to rest well on the night before the show opens in anticipation of the exceptionally long days ahead working the busy booth followed by multiple nights of entertaining those potential clients.

Having already been in town working for an entire week, I was particularly exhausted and anxious to get back to my room for an early dinner and bedtime which was exactly what I did. Good thing, too, because the next morning? Wow. Just wow.

I happened to be in front of the hotel sending off a colleague when a taxi pulled up, and I could not help but stare a bit as the passenger that was slow to get out was still wearing a hospital gown. As the man carefully unfolded from that back seat, I also saw his head was tightly wrapped in an enormous hospital bandage that kind of looked like a bad job of a turban headdress. On further inspection, I realized that under the enlarged-head-wrapped-in-hospital-gauze was one of my sales managers.

"Leo?"

As I approached and came to a full stop with a complete look of shock, my mouth must have gaped open while wondering at closer inspection why that turban of gauze was bundled so tightly around the side of his right ear. Not that I could see any of it. In fact, wait! Was that a drop or two of blood I saw on that side of those multi-folds of bandages? What the…?

"Holy Hannah, Leo!"

I jumped into planner turned mother turned employee concerned with company liability mode and just went into over-drive trying to make sense of things. The mother in me wanted to rush Leo into his room and let him rest, but the planner in me knew I had to ask some hard questions. Unfortunately for Leo (or maybe at that moment in time it was lucky?) he was still woozy from whatever had been administered to him in the hospital and could only supply some vague answers to my rapid-fire round of questions.

"What the heck happened? What is your prognosis here? What kind of medical instructions did they dismiss you with?"

And when the responses were few and guarded, I remembered the gauze was over one ear and considered that maybe speaking louder would help my cause because that always helps, right?

"LEO. LEO! WORK WITH ME! PLEASE?"

After some back-and-forth muttering, I learned that after leaving our team happy hour the night before, he and another employee, Rick, had gone to "a bar or two". Cough. Shock. Surprise. *NOT!*

"And, then what?" I was quickly losing my patience and needed some answers. Apparently the sweet, empathetic mom (me) had switched to an angry one, tapping her foot on the ground as she grilled the irresponsible son for details of his "boys behaving badly" night out.

And oh boy. What a story it was. He "kind of" remembered returning to his hotel room. He also recalled that it was bloody. Very, very bloody in that room.

Oh Lordy. Please help me. Did someone follow him to his room? Was he drugged and robbed? Beat up?

"LEO! Do you know what time it was when you came back here?"

Exceedingly long pause, then "Uh, late. Super late. Maybe this morning?"

He clearly had no idea, although he "maybe" remembered saying goodnight to Rick in the hotel elevator before they parted, each on separate hotel floors.

As I escorted him through the lobby, I was processing a million things at once. If indeed he had a "bloody room", was it a crime scene? Should I take him back there? At some point I started thinking a little more clearly and decided I should first try to check him into a new room, no easy feat during a city-wide convention, and then deal with the original one. *Perhaps, gulp, with a CSI expert?*

Once he was tucked in and resting in that new room, I reached out to the company's Chief Sales and Marketing Officer, Kurt, the ranking employee who was on site with me, and got him involved. Knowing we also had a big important show to kick off within the hour, we came up with a divide and conquer plan to get things done and to organize the chaos ahead. Phone calls were made and a few things got ticked off our list, but as the day progressed things were getting, as Alice in Wonderland would say, "curioser and curioser."

First, we determined that his "partner in crime," Rick, was just fine. Slept well and apparently had no further knowledge of what went on with Leo after they parted. So, Rick was ready to work in the booth which is exactly what we let him do while the investigation continued with the hotel's security team, who at this point had already called the Crime Investigative Unit for the city.

Yes, CIU. *This was actually happening!*

Hotel security escorted us to their downstairs office where we were able to review all the hotel cameras which provided nothing in the way of riveting footage of our dynamic duo. In fact, the only surprise revealed to me in that exercise was exactly how many security cameras were in that hotel. They were everywhere! In reviewing that footage, we did see Rick and Leo (no turban yet) returning to the hotel, walking into the lobby and heading to the elevator, each getting off at his own floor. We saw no one lurking in the hallways. Nothing at all suspicious, that is until we toured the room.

Astounding. And yet even that doesn't seem like a big enough word to describe what we saw.

Blood was everywhere. It was like a crime scene, but we still had no crime.

We walked through everything, every inch of that place. The hotel already had an investigator on this case and after meeting up with him at "the scene of the yet unresolved crime" he shared the few details he had been able to determine.

Apparently, someone in the room (presumably Leo) had knocked the phone off the handset in the middle of the night and tried incoherently to talk to the operator, but they could not understand him. Fortunately for Leo the hotel operator was alert enough to call 911 and that began the process of having security do the necessary follow up. Once in the room and upon discovery of all that blood, the most gruesome part of this story was revealed. The heaviest blood path was by the backside of the door, close to the hinges, and it was there that they found a large chunk of Leo's ear.

Yes, you read that correctly.

Further, finding no signs of a physical struggle with another person or anything missing from his personal belongings it was ultimately determined that this was a case of someone who was clearly under the influence - as in losing all senses - while taking a bad drug trip to trouble with a capital "T" that night.

Further, Leo was so entirely out of it, he had no recollection of what had transpired the night before.

Yep. Apparently, our Leo, even after he was rested, in recovery, and had been shown video tapes and hospital records of his obvious condition that night, was in complete denial. Had no idea what had happened when he returned to his room and no memory of what went on there. We got no mea culpa Vincent Van Gogh confession out of this guy even though he was now, um, minus an ear!

And, after a long couple of days, we put "Van Gogh'" back on a plane to Atlanta in an ultimate embarrassment for a business traveler as he was wearing a tourist sweatshirt we had purchased for his comfort from the local drug store. Yes, minus his pride and very definitely carrying his still-wrapped-in-turban head low with his reputation at risk, he looked more like he got beat-up in a bar brawl and came out missing one ear.

As for the rest of our team over at the show, they never skipped a beat, so for everyone except Leo, that trip would be remembered as a success.

That is, except for me.

As part of my event follow up, I had to process the actual film and photographs taken at the bloody scene and to be honest, to this day I still can't even watch a CSI episode on TV without breaking out in a sweat and feeling just a little queasy. Hands down that turned out to be one of grossest, strangest, and most bizarre events in my career!

Pre-Con Meeting*: This is an inclusive meeting held pre-convention, attended by all the major planners and stakeholders from both the client and service venue in which all aspects of the event are discussed in great detail. In this story it was an employee meeting of those on the sales team that had traveled to the event and would be working their company's booth at the show.

Lessons Learned:

✓ Have an emergency/contingency plan in place that includes details of who to call in case of medical emergency for each of your company's employees. Granted, this was an extraordinary "event", but now that you've read to the end of my story you surely believe that most anything can and will and does happen in the crazy world of meetings and events!

JULIE WILHARM CLARK BIO: Julie is a veteran planner and marketing pro who has learned a thing or two on her storied industry journey through the highs and lows of managing both meetings and extensive marketing campaigns for major corporations all over the world. She says she occasionally wonders how "Leo Van Gogh" is doing these days, but then quickly pours another adult beverage to move on and get her through the next event.

www.creativelyclark.com

Chapter Six

Confetti for Days

By Gladi Colón, CMP

This is one of those stories where I can look back now and laugh at it, but at the time it was happening, I felt that knot in the pit of my stomach feeling, and just wanted to crawl under a rock.

I worked in event management for a hotel company for eleven years. It was a luxury property, one of those where the people constantly fluff the pillows in the lobby and has the luxurious scent of grapefruit and lavender pumping through the air vents. I was proud to work there and proud to follow the rules and standards that were in place, designed to keep the property operating in tip-top condition.

Now that the scene has been set, let me take you back to the night I thought I had squandered my perfect event record and wanted to crawl under a rock. It was the final night of a three-day extravaganza. Yes, extravaganza. Calling this event anything less than, would not do it justice. It was a real spectacle, thousands of professionals under one roof, being wined and dined and completely submerged into the experience. Every moment of the event was Instagramable and unforgettable... including the final night.

At the request of my amazing client, I had hesitantly agreed, last minute, for her staff to put together a "confetti departure" for the attendees. I use the word "hesitant" because if you are in the hotel side of things, you **rarely** agree to anything with confetti because the clean-up is usually a nightmare.

Under normal circumstances I would have needed to run this past the big boss, however, I agreed and without question, because I simply wanted to make my client happy. If this confetti departure, in her eyes would be the icing on the cake, then I figured, what is a few minutes of clean up in the grand scheme of things? After all, she was a repeat client, and I didn't want to say no to something that could be trivial and sour the relationship with the property. We pick our battles and offer flexibility when justified.

Little did I know that in actuality what I had agreed to was over **2,000 individual handheld** confetti canons, each stuffed with hundreds of colorful pieces of confetti. See, in my mind what I was expecting was equivalent to one stage-style confetti canon, the "one blast" and you're done kind of thing, no big deal.

No, this was quite the opposite.

This confetti departure, or as I refer to it now as the confetti *parade,* went on for the longest hour of my career with the constant popping of confetti floating in the air. I stood back from a distance, watching as the floors in the convention center foyer became coated, and the chandeliers now bedazzled with rainbow-colored confetti. There were confetti pieces in the window treatments, the crown molding, all the hard-to-reach places! There was so much confetti, I recall it got to about 6 inches thick, like snow. And like snow, when you walk through it, it travels with you.

My heart started to pound out of my chest. A few things ran through my mind.

How was I going to clean this up? It is late and almost everyone has gone home already.

How are my bosses going to take this? Am I going to get coached?

Was it worth it?

Then as the last few people trickled out, and that one guy finished doing snow-angels, I looked around and saw my client in the distance with the biggest smile on her face.

Suddenly, my anxiety levels were lower, and I felt a wave of calmness come over me. At that moment I realized it did not matter how I was going to clean it up or explain to my boss why we were still finding pieces of confetti weeks later in the once immaculate conference center. What mattered is that smile in the distance.

I pride myself on following the rules but at the same time, knowing when to bend them. It took a few volunteers (me begging friends to stay later), a case of Red bull energy drinks, and a little over four hours to clean the mess. But this time I am glad I bent the rules as it meant creating lasting memories not just for my client, but for the thousands of conference attendees who became raving fans after this experience.

Fun fact: the best tool we found for piling up the confetti were several rubber squeegee brooms from the dish room. So now you know!

The next morning, I came clean to my bosses about what transpired the night before. They laughed and surprisingly to them, it was not a big deal after all, or perhaps I'm now just explaining for the first time the gravity of the situation.

At any rate, it is times like these that I'm reminded why we empower our teams in the first place, so they can, without doubt, make a decision and stick with it, even if it means going against the grain. Next time, I will be sure to ask for specifics on the canons before committing, but the more important lesson here is I'm glad I went with my gut because, in the end, it was all worth it.

GLADI COLON BIO: Originally from Melbourne, Florida, Gladi now resides in Orlando, Florida where she built her career in hospitality and event management. She is the Director of Event Management at the 1,335 room Caribe Royale Orlando Resort and Co-Founder of H&F Redefined, a promotional network supporting colleagues and peers through their furlough and new business journeys. Gladi is a proud graduate of the University of Central Florida, Rosen College of Hospitality, and enjoys cheering on the Knights.

https://www.hfredefined.com/

CHAPTER SEVEN

That Time My Stage Floor Caved in Right Before Patti LaBelle's Performance

By Paul Creighton, CSEP

It was the type of business that Orlando lives for. A successful multi-level marketing company coming to town and looking for an over-the-top final evening outside their hotel. Every company in town was chasing after the business.

The winning company was a décor company who pitched the idea of a multi-tiered tent with hard wood floors and hard walls overlooking a lake in the posh town of Windermere just outside Orlando. The highlight of their pitch was revealing Barry Manilow sitting at a piano in the middle of the lake on a platform. In the pitch, after the reveal the platform would move with Barry still performing, "musically floating" towards the tent filled with guests and then seamlessly merge with the existing stage docked on land that housed a twenty-piece orchestra. Once Barry's dramatic entrance was complete, the show would continue, and the guests would have their unforgettable memory.

As it turned out, the guests got their unforgettable memory, just not the one they expected.

Our company was approached early in the negotiations to provide the various non-headliner entertainment that would be featured. Sadly, as we learned more about the occasion, it became apparent that the décor company had never even checked to see if Barry Manilow would agree to that kind of floating entrance-he wouldn't-so that should have been our first red flag. Undeterred by that setback, they moved on Dolly Parton who also took a pass. The event producer finally struck gold when Patti Labelle agreed, but this type of back-and-forth exchange heightened our awareness that we needed to make sure our end of the event (the twenty-piece orchestra with vocalist, a small jazz quartet, and several solo piano players for the entrance) was buttoned down tight.

On the day of the show, I arrived on site at noon to over-see the orchestra load-in. What I found was nothing less than chaos. There had been steady rain showers for the past three days (welcome to Florida), and clearly the décor company was running behind schedule, not to mention the entire area was mucky, murky, and definitely muddy. The tent structure (located lakeside, at the bottom of a hill) was upright but nowhere near dressed out. But what was even more alarming and really caught my now quite disturbed attention, was witnessing staff running helter-skelter everywhere attempting to get furniture and carpeting down what was now an impossibly muddy path-way into the tent. I would compare it to a comedy routine from a Marx Brothers film except this was real and I was in the thick of it so really found nothing to laugh about. At all!

Wanting to assist I asked the décor company how I could help and found myself joining in on the bedlam while spending the next four hours carrying heavy rolls of carpet down that rain-soaked hill. This is where I should also mention that during this entire time the end client's in-house planner who had come over to supervise her very expensive set for the night's big event was more than a little unhappy. And "unhappy" might be an understatement, so let's tell it like it really was. She. Was. Furious.

I mean screaming at the top of her lungs for the benefit of anyone who would listen, which of course was all of us because we were stuck in the middle of this mayhem. First it was, "I am suing YOU for this!" followed quickly by, "You'll never work in this town again!". And then everyone's favorite and always a motivator when you want people to work harder, "If you don't get this finished in the next three hours, *I'm not paying you!*" Yes, those were just a few of the high-volume outbursts that I heard. Oh boy!

Obviously, everyone working on site was aware of what was going on and tensions were soaring. But miraculously by the time the busses started arriving, it "appeared" that everything was in place and ready to go. The guests, anticipating an exciting evening full of great entertainment and company surprises, took their seats inside the tent as a jazz quartet played lively walk-in music to help set the tone. After cleaning up and refocusing on the task at hand, which was to deliver a good show, I took my place near the sound console and surprise! I realized that sitting next to me was the less-than-friendly in-house planner who at this point seemed, if not calm, at least accepting that somehow this "blankety-blank motley crew" had managed to pull things together and that maybe, just maybe, tonight would actually happen as planned.

If only!

In fairness, things were going smoothly at the start. That is until we heard that first mysterious and very loud crack-bang

(!) as it pierced the room. It was the distinct sound of a board splintering, and in a split second we could see that part of the flooring under a table had given way causing that table to quickly sink onto the floor.

Yes.

Full stop here as you picture that there were people seated at this table and the table itself was fully dressed out with china, glasses, linens, etc. Oh, and those occupied chairs? Yes, they went down too.

Now do you have the full visual of shock and awe?

Add to that the "enthusiastic" shouts of those guests as they plunged. And before the stunned crowd could fully register what was happening with that table, BANG! Another crack from another side of the room, followed by, well, you guessed it. More tables falling, china breaking, and people tumbling. One right after another and yes, it was now happening in multiple areas all over.

Cue the pandemonium!

On the plus side (if there was one to be found), the floors-even on the higher levels of elevation-were no more than four to five feet off the ground, so no one was seriously injured. However, the room was most definitely in full panic mode at this point.

As the chaos continued, at some point a loud voice finally took command to silence the crowd. A man yelled "STOP", and miraculously the people did. Turns out it was the recognizable and mesmerizing voice of the founder of the company which, if you know anything about multi-level marketing events, when the leader speaks, silence follows. So yes, even without a mic, he immediately got the full attention of the now panicked crowd.

"Listen up, people! We are (company name here). We do not act this way. We've obviously had an accident, but here is what we're going to do. We are all going to leave this tent in an orderly fashion, and we are going to get back on the busses and return to our hotel. And when we get there, we are going to do what we always do. We're going to open our wallets and make ourselves a party!"

And amazingly, that is exactly what happened.

As the guests filed out, I turned to the in-house planner and tepidly asked what she wanted to do. To my surprise there was no answer. She was frozen in disbelief and speechless, so I sprang into action and started formulating a plan.

I already knew that the hotel these guests were headed back to was a property with which my company had already secured an established and good working relationship. Without waiting for the stunned planner's permission, I called the hotel front desk and asked for the general manager. At first I was told that he was off property and couldn't be bothered. But I persisted and explained to the manager that approximately 800 guests were about to arrive (I wisely avoided using the phrase "traumatized, in shock and needing adult beverages") and they were going to be looking for a party, so he had better get in touch with the general manager right away because he would definitely want to know.

Next, I went to the orchestra and talked to the leader. I took a deep breath and explained that he had no obligation to do this, but if he could convince the band to quickly tear down and head to the hotel to play for the guests over there it would be a good gesture. After what had just taken place, it did take a little convincing before he reluctantly agreed, so I can't say that I blamed him for being a bit skeptical about what might lie ahead. In turn, most of the orchestra members–those that still had their wits about them-signed on as well.

When we arrived at the hotel, I was relieved to learn that my advance warning call to the general manager had been taken seriously. There was already a ballroom being set with tables and chairs and the only open dining spot in the hotel that evening, a Chinese restaurant, was already busy delivering pans of lo Mein to the ballroom. Plus, during the bus ride back to the hotel the client had called Dominos to order a couple hundred pizzas. But the real surprise was that the client executives had stopped at a liquor store and bought every bottle of Dom Perignon that they could get their hands on making Dom, Dominos and Lo Mein the featured meal for the evening. Too bad their planner went AWOL for the rest of the night (to the surprise of no one...) as I'm certain we could have shocked her one more time with that odd combination of food and alcohol!

And I was so proud to assist my orchestra as they quickly got set up and began playing music at the same time that pizzas started flying and champagne corks were popping because in the end, we were able to provide a particularly good platform for those weary guests to let loose and have some fun at long last.

At some point during what turned out to be a wild and wonderful party, a company representative came up and asked if the band would be willing to perform overtime because everyone was finally letting loose and having a blast. I had no choice but to speak frankly in explaining we would be happy to do it, but I was concerned about payment. Given the circumstances it seemed likely that there would be financial disagreements between the client and the décor company (our client) which was going to jeopardize our getting paid. But I then proposed that if they would agree to pay us directly for the band, we would agree to do the overtime. The client was eager to amicably negotiate and thinking back now on that evening I don't even remember how late that party went. But later, I did learn that with everyone else striking gear from the tent as the guests departed, we were the only vendor that came back to the hotel with the client so that had made a great impression on them.

And regarding Ms. LaBelle and her ill-fated performance on that floating dock, I did hear that the client begged to get her to come back with us all to do a proper performance at the hotel that night. But, and this will come as no surprise to anyone who has dealt with celebrities of this caliber, that was a hard no. She wasn't about to put her reputation on the line (again) without her proper gear and necessary soundcheck. Apparently, that "grand opening calamity" had been enough excitement for one night as far as they were concerned. Further negotiating was a no-win situation from the start of "would Ms. LaBelle consider…?"

In the end, those guests ultimately had a spontaneous and marvelous time. Additionally, everyone-minus those with a few minor cuts, scrapes, and bruises-had a great story they would be telling for years to come, so at least something positive came from that disastrous beginning!

Lessons Learned:

✓ **Do not promise more than you can deliver.** The décor company was over their head from the very beginning, and they obviously overestimated their capabilities. It was a good lesson for everyone in Orlando, at the time a still growing convention town, because there were many companies chasing after this large and attractive piece of business. How many of them would have over-promised to get the business? I'm guessing more than a few.

As a wrap-up to this portion, it turned out that the reason the floor caved in was that due to the three days of rain leading up to the event, the décor company cut corners on the floor install. They only hammered in every third brace. As the footers sunk into the mud, the braces gave way, and the rest is now event history.

✓ **Karma Matters** – there is no proof, but I am absolutely convinced that the angry planner's negative energy and threatening management style certainly contributed to the problem on site. This is a spiritual thing, but I believe that event professionals are supposed to bring calm to an event, not add to the chaos. She did none of that, and when things unraveled, so did she.

✓ **When a problem comes up, fix the problem first, then argue about what went wrong.** We could have stayed at the tent and dissected what happened, but instead, we helped keep the party going by expediting the orchestra's strike in order to move to the new location. We were under no contractual obligation to do so, but it seemed like the right thing to do and at that point, there really was a collective team effort from my group to salvage whatever we could from this disaster. This ended up being a huge move for us because the client did NOT pay the décor company for the job and ended up suing them, ultimately into bankruptcy.

AUTHOR'S FINAL SIDENOTE: On the plus side and as mentioned above because my company had gone the extra step, the client agreed to pay us directly. And when all was finally said and done, we learned we were actually the only company that got paid on the job and not just for the orchestra members that came back to perform at the hotel but for ALL of the entertainment we had contracted. Yes, it was a good feeling for my team but sadly the only plus from an extremely dramatic, stress-filled and unfortunate evening.

PAUL CREIGHTON BIO: Paul is the Executive Vice-President of T. Skorman Productions, Inc, one of the largest entertainment producers in the country. A winner of numerous industry awards, including the Special Event Lifetime Achievement Gala Award, Paul specializes in creating general session entertainment, producing headline entertainment, and managing regional and national corporate entertainment acts. A 24-year member of ILEA, Paul is a vocal proponent of the need for continuing education in the industry.

www.tskorman.com

Chapter Eight

Is That a Stripper on My Stage?

As told to tml by Sharon Fisher

author special note: *This challenging situation happened in the mid 1980's, a time when business protocol was much different than it is now. To be clear, what might have been viewed as a practical joke back then would probably/most likely end up in a nasty lawsuit in this age of diversity and gender discrimination. Just sayin'...*

This story falls under the category of "always do what the customer wants...except when you have a sneaking suspicion that you shouldn't."

Like many others before me, early in my career I learned that there is an awful lot of on-the-job learning in this industry, and the situation I'm telling you about today is one of those.

I was maybe five years out of school working at a super cool high-end beach resort as the Recreation Director. This was my first job in the private sector. In the beginning, my job consisted mostly of taking care of the resort's social guests, making sure the activity calendar was always full of fun events for every age group, and we did have a lot to offer at this location. But as the resort popularity increased, I found myself drawn into more and more work with the convention groups that were checking in for multiple days. And to be honest, this was a completely new market for me but one I jumped into with open arms. I quickly found my groove planning wacky Olympics and treasure hunts on the beach which back then was still relatively new for these groups. But no matter what I did, it was definitely OJT for me at that point because my boss, a rather cool but a bit mysterious man, was kind of a "no talky to me too muchy" type of guy. This is worth mentioning because it helps to put the rest of my story into perspective.

One day the Director of Resort Sales brought an important client to me so we could discuss an upcoming group's need for a spouse program. And when I say "we" I mean it was really just myself and the client in this discussion during which time I quickly learned this was an especially important piece of business for our resort. It was obvious that everyone on staff was doing whatever we needed to keep the client happy which, in turn, meant repeat business for our resort. So, follow along with this dialogue as it took place during my first meeting with the group CEO.

CLIENT: We need about a two-hour program for our ladies while my guys are in a meeting, and I already know exactly what I want.

ME: GREAT! And what is that?

CLIENT: I want a color analyst. You know, one of those gals that does all that stuff for the gals about fashion dos and don'ts and color wheels. All that jazz.

ME: (in my head thinking I have no idea what he's talking about but answering) Great! I'll get right on it and book you someone perfect.

And that was that.

After a long and extensive search – remember, this was all new to me – I finally felt I had found the perfect woman to do this presentation. She was very polished and professional, had perfect posture and make up, and was so well spoken her voice just mesmerized me. So yes, basically the exact opposite of me, the twenty-something-year-old recreation gal fresh out of school who, up until this point, was usually managing treasure hunts on the beach for the kiddos.

So, her contract was confirmed and the client, who by now I had learned was proving to be a bit out-of-the-box, you might even say wild and crazy, approved of everything as we moved through the planning process. But imagine my surprise when one week prior to the event I get a call from the client that went something like this.

ME: Hi there! What can I help you with today?

CLIENT: Well, I've got to add a little surprise to that program for the ladies.

ME: Great! What do you want to surprise them with? Spa appointments? Champagne brunch?

CLIENT: A male stripper.

ME: (Silence. Is he pulling my chain here?)

CLIENT: Sharon, you got that?

ME: Um, yes? But can you tell me more?

CLIENT: Every year we do this meeting, and every year I surprise the ladies with *something!* Trust me, they expect something weird, and they will think this is hilarious!

Then he went on to explain very specifically that he still wanted the color expert to start her program but then the stripper would interrupt by bursting into the scene and do 'his thing.'

Okay then, let's find ourselves a stripper!

I must confess I spent quite a bit of time deliberating whether or not I should repeat this conversation with my boss (remember him? The guy who didn't like to talk?) before deciding no. I should just act like a confident adult and do exactly what the customer wants because after all, that's our motto here, right?!

And with only five days before this group's arrival (not to mention ZERO experience in booking a stripper!), I diligently began my research which basically amounted to me asking everyone I knew (quietly, definitely on the QT) for advice and contacts.

Fun fact here in case you are wondering. After conducting that "extensive research" on my part, the consensus was it is much easier to locate and hire a female stripper than a male... just saying. Oh, and imagine my surprise in learning that the pricing for said stripper was almost the same as for the professional speaker!

Anyway, once that task was accomplished, I had to go through another round of negotiations with our professional speaker because, well let's just say she was not happy about playing along with this kind of shenanigans. At. All. Even despite the fact that she would still be paid in full she made it clear she was not at all comfortable with this arrangement which basically made two of us thinking the same thing.

So, back to the client I went only to find out that *he* wasn't accepting of *her* pushback, either. At. All. I won't repeat the conversation but trust me when I tell you that in the end the client got exactly what he wanted which was a professional speaker to start the program followed by, well, let's cut to the chase and tell you how it all came down on that fateful day in my early career.

Our prim-and-oh-so-proper color analyst dressed in her best professional attire with hair coiffed just so and coordinating nail tips and accessories everywhere began her presentation by cordially greeting her all-female audience. This was promptly interrupted when I, nervously positioned in the back of the room, pressed play on the boom box while my other "professional entertainer" casually made an entrance strolling down the middle aisle until he took his place on the stage at which time he proceeded to do his "*thang.*"

This is the point where speaker No. 1 abruptly left the stage and walked to the very back of the room to quickly distance herself from this distasteful mayhem. This is also the point at which the audience went silent. Actually stunned is a better word, and even that might not be a good description.

Yep. Instead of playing along and accepting that a gag was happening in front of them they were horrified. But not as much as me! I honestly think they thought it was part of the program, and yet they couldn't quite connect the dots between a color coordinator and a stripper.

As if there really were any.

In all honestly – and possibly naivety on my part - I'm not exactly sure what I expected from this group of spouses. Hootin' and hollerin'? Ladies jumping up on stage to join in on the action? This was most definitely out of my wheelhouse, especially given that 'hefty' five years of on-the-job experience my resume was showing.

Plus, hadn't that "crazy VIP client" said, "they'll love it!" when he insisted that I book the stripper? Oh yes, he had! But come to think of it, where the heck was he right now? Certainly not in this room at this moment in time. And the ladies DEFINITELY didn't think it was hilarious.

From my position in back of the room (there was no closet I could crawl into) I agonized while watching the train wreck happening up front until I could no longer stand it. I don't actually know whether it was a New York minute or a full fifteen before I summoned up all my youthful courage to yell "STOP!" I followed that with the uniform sign language of a sharp slice to my throat as I marched toward the stage to cut him off. Then this.

STRIPPER TO ME: But I didn't finish!

ME: OH YEAH, PRETTY SURE YOU DID!

The rest of this story is (gratefully) a bit of a blur, but I do remember that somehow I managed to blubber out a brief explanation to the still-in-shock audience who finally gave a somewhat guarded but definite chuckle at the whole ordeal. At least that's the way I choose to remember it now.

Oh, and after all that excitement, our color analyst was somehow able to compose herself, and the audience, enough to finish her program with her wits still intact and her perfectly coiffed head held high. A sign of a true professional, which is more than I could say for that stripper who really, really wanted to finish what he was hired to do!

In the end, the guests left somewhat happy, clutching their color charts, but also with definite confusion about what they had just witnessed.

And as for my boss?

He just laughed hysterically and said, "thank you for taking such good care of our client."

Lessons Learned:

✓ Even when the client requests that you do so, DO NOT hire strippers for your event. It's never gonna end well.

✓ And dare I say that contrary to what you are usually taught, just because they are the client does not mean they are always right.

As an aside, this lesson has been proven to me time and again in my (now) lengthy industry career, but at some point in the learning curve you do learn to speak up. As of this writing I'm still waiting for another client to request a stripper to tuck into their event because, well, I'm anxious to set the record straight on what a very, VERY bad idea that would be!

SHARON FISHER BIO: As the CEO and Chief Idea Sparker of Play With a Purpose, an Orlando based company focusing on creative and unique corporate engagement, Sharon has come a long way since her early days of staging beachside treasure hunts and hiring strippers to 'tuck' into spouse programs. As one of the true pioneers of providing revolutionary event experiences for corporations all over the globe, Sharon is now also a sought-after speaker who vows to "never stop playing."

www.playwithapurpose.com

CHAPTER NINE

Problem Solving Canadian Style

By Sandi Galloway, CPECP

I was working as Director of Meetings, Conventions & Incentive Travel for the Canadian Tourism Commission and had about a ten-month lead to plan a client event for my Canadian partners who wanted to attract more US business. It had to be something special that would allow us (a variety of Canadian hotels, **DMCs***, **CVBs***, and such) to highlight some uniquely Canadian elements in order to convince some US based meeting planners to bring more convention business to their friendly neighbors up North.

This event was to be held in Dallas, and I was fortunate to find a restaurant owned by Canadians that were willing to work with us for an incredibly special evening. After some back-and-forth creative brainstorming, they agreed to allow me to bring in four Executive Chefs from top hotels across Canada who would authentically feature Canadian cuisine. As always happens when planning these events, the excitement was building as we worked through the planning stages and added more distinctive touches, all with the goal of showcasing Canada as a top-notch location for meetings and incentive business coming across the border. Our invitee list was completed, and an artistic "Save the Date" card was sent out to help build anticipation for what we hoped would be a wonderful evening for our guests.

So, imagine my shock when about six weeks out I received a call telling me that the restaurant owners had filed for divorce and were closing the restaurant!

Say what?

Or in Canadian terms, "eh?"

In addition to all the décor and theme planning that had been reserved and confirmed, airline tickets for over twenty of my partners plus the four "celebrity" chefs, all flying in from Canada, had already been purchased! Once the astonishment of that announcement sunk in, I immediately started calling numerous other restaurants and hotels, but not one would let chefs from other hotels into their kitchens and having those highly recognizable guest chefs had already been announced as the focal point of our event. So much for across-the-border détente!

So, my meeting planner and I called an emergency session with a couple of industry colleagues to see how we could salvage the event while staying within our budget, time frame, and already announced expectations. This is where meeting planning skills and industry networking really pays off!

In a truly short time frame, here is what we rallied to confirm:

- Moved the event to a local film studio. We were able to use the exact space we needed by moving the floor-to-ceiling black curtains to create a more intimate space which was simply perfect for our needs.

- Worked with a local culinary school and that proved to be a lifesaver! They provided all the food prep items, chaffing dishes, etc., plus we were able to entice several students to work for free in exchange for a recommendation letter from the Executive Chef that they were assigned to work with the night of the event. The students were extremely excited for this real-life experience and the Chefs got some great helpers. A win-win!

- Used the event planning department at a specialty grocery store to obtain all the extremely specific food items needed by our chefs who, as you remember, were focusing on Canadian cuisine.

- An industry event décor friend was able to get us "reject linens" (which had definitely seen better days) from a linen rental company. But we used them on the buffet display so by artistically scrunching and draping them we were able to cover those holes and stains, so no one ever suspected they were rejects. Since the studio already had black drapes surrounding the walls and great rigging, a lighting consultant suggested using gobo lights to create a Canadian winter theme with snowflakes rotating and floating around the room. To that we added pin lights on the buffet as well as spotlights over our chef stations. No one ever knew that most of our winter décor came from Hobby Lobby and The Dollar Tree. The budget was small, but the look was stunning!

- Best of all, our printer was able to rework the invitations to make them fit our new theme and location at no additional cost, plus we were able to get them out on time. No small accomplishment.

In the end, the event went off with only one little glitch that we learned the hard way: NEVER use a snow machine inside a building. We had to turn it off just minutes after starting it after quickly discovering that the fumes were toxic!

The final result was an evening that our clients loved and talked about for a long time, and one that I personally will never forget. Mostly for the good parts, but definitely for those challenging ones, too!

*__DMC definition:__ Destination Management Company. These are for profit companies located in major tourist areas worldwide and provide valuable services such as connecting meeting planners with solutions to meet their travel, meeting, and entertainment interests as they pertain to that local community.

*__CVB definition:__ Convention & Visitor Bureau. These are usually government funded (via hotel and/or tourist taxes) and represent all local entities (attractions, restaurants, hotels, and more) in their overall marketing and public relations efforts with the goal of increasing visitors to that destination.

SANDI GALLOWAY BIO: Sandi, an industry veteran, spent her first twenty years traveling the world working with international airlines including Pan Am and British Airways. She then joined the Canadian Tourism Commission as Director of Meetings, Conventions & Incentive Travel, Southern USA market. She has earned her Certified Protocol, Etiquette & Civility Professional designation (CPECP) from the Global

PEC Academy in Dallas, TX. In recent years she has started her own company specializing in training the hospitality industry in etiquette and travel safety, mentoring many newbies on the journey ahead.

https://www.linkedin.com/in/sandi-galloway-cpecp-a631167/

Chapter Ten

From Glitch to Glory

By Laura Hartmann, PBC, CPCE

I had been waiting for this day for eight long months. It was finally here. All the planning, innovating, tastings, design, training, detail work and let's face it, HEART was about to be exposed to our 2300 VIP guests. Nothing could go wrong.

Until it did.

On day one.

Let me rewind, so you can understand how I got here. Sweating and shaking profusely on the convention floor is what I mean by "here."

As the Assistant Director of Events for a big box convention property, I would be taking the lead on managing and executing the food and beverage events for our hotel company's General Manager conference. This conference is like the "super bowl" of programs for any hotel to take on. The pressure to perform individually, and as a team, while representing your property to the entire company leadership team is intense. Don't get me wrong, it's a true honor to host this conference, however quite the beast to execute.

It was important to me and our team to ensure that every single food and beverage function truly felt like an experience, deliver a message, and have purpose. This included the AM/PM breaks. We could have taken the easy route and put all of our energy and focus into the big specialty evening events, however we considered this a "legacy" project due to the scale and scope of the program.

You DON'T settle for half-ass on a legacy project.

Unlike many programs that open with a welcome reception, we had a unique flow to work with and our first actual food and beverage event was an afternoon break. BORING! However, this was a VVIP pre-meeting of a select group of 350 company leaders attending an opening session lead by none other but the President of the America's for our MAJOR Hotel brand. The rest of the 2000 attendees were trickling in and would get their big wow experience at the welcome event that evening, but these 350 executives… well, I could not forget them or their extremely valued and often critical opinions of their first impression.

The theme we finally landed on was called the "Welcome Home" break. We decided to connect a corporate initiative that the President was deeply passionate about (employing military veterans) with our food and beverage experience by showcasing our OWN property vets. We had them each submit the one snack item they missed the most while deployed, and then we artfully designed a menu around those responses to serve at this break.

Our veterans would also be there, standing at attention in two rows, with camouflage company branded hats, ready to greet the attendees as they all would break simultaneously from the general session room. A giant 8'x9' custom menu chalkboard would anchor the foyer space, featuring quotes from the vets' response sheets, bringing their collaboration right into the food display. Powerful.

We designed the entire foyer space to have a retro/vintage feel, with a few modern techy twists, and wanted it to be perfect not only for the attendees but also the veterans that deserved a polished presentation.

One of the "modern techy twists" were six LED 6ft-tall vertical sign boards. I was obsessed with these boards. The boards are usually used for wayfinding, or displaying general content such as program agendas, however I saw an opportunity to integrate them into our overall design plan for the full program week. For the most part, I would be using them as six individual boards, however, for the "Welcome Home" break, I was going to have them all in a row with the content synched together to create one wavering American flag that overlays across the group of panels. Stunning and such a super cool effect.

Event day arrives, we are ready to go. Setup begins and I am balancing my time between the extensive outdoor welcome reception setup for later that night, and this opening afternoon break. There are vendors everywhere, three camera crews following us, corporate execs checking in on us, and an army-sized operations team marching like ants, dividing and conquering, and blowing up my phone every other second.

In the midst of all the organized chaos, I headed back of house to the audio visual war room to check out my beloved LED screens, as I hadn't seen them yet and was excited to see this flag effect in action.

They were everything I had hoped for, and I knew they would be an impressive wow factor aligning with the conference theme of "the next 100 years" and a centennial, futuristic vibe.

The techs set up the screens to show me the animation effect and all was looking perfect. However, as I started to chat with a colleague, something kept catching my attention about the screens in the corner of my eye. One of the panels was glitching. Like an obvious glitch.

I started to panic, as I knew something was wrong and I would need to have these fixed ASAP because a technical glitch like this would not look professional. Remember that part about not settling?

I got a team on the problem right away, however after much troubleshooting, the LED screens would not sync with one another properly and the more they messed with it the worse it got. It went from half a flag, to no flag, to a quarter of a flag, on and on.

Of course, I had planned for them to be positioned directly outside of the doors on the perfect angle so each guest would no doubt get that wow moment of the crisp, clear, technology in front of them. But unless it got fixed, as it was right now, they would be shielding their eyes or seizing from the sporadic pops of light coming at them.

As we neared closer to event time-mind you at this point attendees are inside the ballroom in session-I realized a backup plan was needed. The AV team rolled out a large plasma television screen on wheels. Gross. Old-school. This is not at all a representation of the "future," nope, we are now going back in time! Nevertheless, it was a contingency plan to have in place while the tech team continued to troubleshoot those six LED screens.

Various vendors started jumping in after seeing me pace around the foyer. I just started sending anyone in a black AV uniform to the war room to look at these things and put their techy heads together regardless of what company they were with. They kept giving me all kinds of updates about what the problem was, hoping I would tell them to just give up and we will proceed with the ugly plasma on wheels. Unfortunately for them they were dealing with the most stubborn perfectionist possible in this scenario, who was personally holding the weight of the success of this entire week on her shoulders (by the way, not recommended). When I have a vision, and my mind is made up on something, it is pretty much pointless even attempting to talk me out of it. Keep troubleshooting guys!

I guess you could say the addict inside me loves the adrenaline rush of the hustle and scramble of getting everything perfect down to the very last second. I mean let's not act like "set and ready fifteen minutes prior" is actually a reality for a program like this. Every minute and every second that you have until those doors open to fine tune the details is what can end up making or breaking the experience.

Finally, my phone rings. "We fixed it!" the lead tech exclaims. Hallelujah!

And then I realize there are only five minutes until doors open. Could we make the swap so quickly? What if they break early?

DOOO IT. I closed my eyes and thought, followed by *"did I really just make that call?"*

The poor techs came running through the halls, each carrying an LED screen. I remember watching them lugging the screens with such commitment. They had never even met me until hours prior and could have several times told me to go pound sand. For some reason though, they were in it with me.

The crowd had now officially built in the foyer (remember there were twenty to thirty veterans ready to stand at attention), and a plethora of other staff. I think half the property was now as emotionally invested in this LED screen initiative as I was. We all watched in suspense as the ugly plasma was rolled away, and they scrambled to set the beauties.

We start to hear the applause inside. NO, the screens were not on yet! Now I've just put us in a position where we could have a big black blank screen, even worse than the old clackety plasma! At least that thing had *content* on it.

I am dying inside, and about to pee my pants while everyone is looking back and forth between me and the LED screens. The applause continues, and then eureka! The screens turn on. YAY!!!

Except then, glitch, glitch glitchity glitch. Here we go again. Dark. My heart sank. I could literally now hear the guests getting up from their chairs. What was I thinking pushing everyone to this level?

And at that moment, I heard a POP from the screens, followed by a KABOOOOM of the ballroom doors busting open. And then gasps from the guests taking in the most glorious digitally animated waving American flag they had ever seen. (At least in my mind that is what they were thinking.)

Someone above was watching over me at that moment. Those screens literally popped back into action the very second those doors busted open. No one knew the wiser. I hugged the wall, and cried, laughed, cried, you know that ugly combination where you are so confused on what has just happened to you?

So, was it worth it? YES. And the rest of the week followed suit to the same tune of "down to the wire" fine tuning and making tweaks to take each experience one step further. That is what we do for our guests. When we know it could be better, then shouldn't it be?

This experience solidified my mindset about never settling, and how important it is to push yourself, push your team, live a little dangerously because that feeling of getting it RIGHT sticks with you forever.

No risk, no reward, no Glory.

LAURA HARTMANN BIO: Originally from Columbia, Missouri, Laura now resides in Orlando, Florida where she built her career in hospitality and event management. Laura graduated from the UCF Rosen College of Hospitality. While in Orlando, she has worked various positions within the industry across brands such as Marriott, Starwood, Hilton and Waldorf Astoria as Assistant Director of Event Management. Most recently she is now the proud Co-Founder of H&F Redefined, a promotional network supporting colleagues and peers through their furlough and new business journeys. She loves illustrating the stories of their successes as well as her own personal correlations to mom and career life through writing and blogging.

https://www.hfredefined.com/

CHAPTER ELEVEN

The Night Hell Froze Over in Texas

By Cindy Hartner, CSEP

Our Destination Management Company (DMC) helped plan an incredible event for a celebrity athlete during the Final Four Tournament in a large, open Dallas warehouse venue for which you needed to bring in all the infrastructure. The event was largely planned through the athlete's non-profit organization which meant, if you're familiar with this type of work, that the planning process was high-level (think famous athletes calling in favors), highly negotiated (non-profit basically means "hey, we can't pay very much but your exposure to other potential business will be fabulous!"), and thoroughly vetted.

Except that nobody could have predicted the rare ice storm in Texas which happened on the first night of the tournament throwing a wrench in many of those details.

Regardless of all the area weather forecasters predicting a "horrible night ahead" due to the impending ice storm, our client was determined their program would move forward. So, all day vendors were scrambling to load in early and get back out on the road before the worst of the storm hit. But at some point in that crazy weather afternoon, many vendors abandoned their commitment and turned their vehicles around because they simply could not make it all the way to the venue without risking life and limb traveling the now-dangerous roads.

So, if you are a planner and keeping track, this is the point where my team was rigorously huddled to work on plans B and then C for all those missing services. Sound familiar?

And while we were scrambling to cover those already identified missing bases, we also discovered that somehow a valet parking service had never even been contracted, a big miss for sure when you're dealing with celebrity events. Oops! Further bad news came when we realized that with all the other big-ticket programs going on simultaneously in the city, mostly connected with the Final Four, it would be impossible at this point to find an available company, especially during this ice storm.

We jumped into even higher gear calling every available body to do us a favor and somehow managed to cobble together a motley crew to do the job. We did have a couple of professional leaders, but the rest were friends, family, and people who owed us favors. Basically, anyone that could get to our venue and was able to park a car.

Yeah, a real liability insurance nightmare!

And even though the entire event was extremely late when it actually got started (did I mention the gloom and doom of that ice storm?), over 2500 guests–primarily elite athletes and celebrities–somehow managed to attend that night. And not a one of them realized that the actual owners of my company were out shoveling snow from the entryway as fast as they could after each and every guest walked a now-invisible red carpet. But that's show biz, right?

Other "fun" things happened, too, like finding out the rest-rooms had completely frozen early in the evening. Joy!

Then at one point during critical communication time (as in "I need help NOW because..."), I accidentally dropped my never-leave-your-side mandatory planning aide - which back then was an on-site radio-into a snow drift never to be found again. Although I'm sure days later when the thaw finally happened some random person made an unusual and puzzling discovery.

Anyway, it was a night to remember, and if you are reading this story and also happen to work in this industry, you know these surprise challenges come up and you always, always rise to the occasion. Or, as in our case, rise above the snow drifts.

Our (frozen) team continued to make adjustments to the original timeline and game plans all night long as we dealt with whatever obstacle that storm blew our way. The end result was a remarkable event, one in which the guests were largely unimpacted (once they made it inside the building), frozen restrooms aside.

When it was all over, I'm quite sure my team slept for about two days following strike that night. Plus, we all had some great stories to tell for years to come about what happened to our event during that "dark and stormy random Texas ice storm!'

Lessons Learned:

✓ Working with celebrities–of any caliber-brings its' own set of challenges and requires a different planning mindset. This is especially true when dealing with non-profit events or entities. Even when the client tells you "they've taken care of that," if you are ultimately in charge of the overall event you must insist on having full disclosure about all contractors and make your own inquiries with each one of them to assure they are on board with providing what you've been told they would provide.

✓ Working with weather surprises is the bane of existence for many events. As you saw in the above story, even though the actual event took place inside a warehouse, that ice storm wreaked havoc on the timely delivery of necessary supplies that were needed to support the overall event. We now make a practice of checking weather advisories with plenty of advance notice!

CINDY HARTNER BIO: When you reach 30 years in the hospitality industry, should you just stop counting? Clients say that Cindy brings a sense of collaboration, sincerity, resourcefulness, enthusiasm, and humor to their programs. In 2019 Cindy published her book, *"You Don't Get a Map, You Get a Compass,"* which is designed to help anybody who has hit a dark place or transition in their life. It is a story of hope, courage and determination told with humor and humility. Cindy is a Texan-living-in-Seattle. Her three adult children live across the country in Washington, Texas and Louisiana striving to be productive, contributing citizens.

https://www.cindyhartner.com/

CHAPTER TWELVE

Mickey Rooney, Boxer Shorts, and Burgers

As told to tml by Sue King

L ife as a Senior Event Planning Manager at a major city-wide convention headquarter hotel for twenty years has included some delightful opportunities that involved celebrity housing. Some have become favorite "wine down" stories following long days of servicing meetings, and this is one.

Our city, Orlando, was hosting a major retired military organization's annual convention of approximately 10,000 attendees and as always, their long-time meeting planner, Ms. V, had spent countless hours, weeks, and months preparing for this important gathering. For me personally, working with military events is always an honor, but this particular convention was a major anniversary year so they were pulling out all the stops and paying tribute to the United Service Organization, known the world over as the USO. Further, they had picked two of their top celebrities, Mikey Rooney and Ann Margaret, to honor at this convention, both with storied careers involving countless tours to entertain US Troops stationed all over the world (including inside active war zones), and I was tickled to learn the honorees would be staying in our hotel.

Ms. Ann Margaret arrived with little fan fair, floating across our front drive like a vision in an emerald-tone cloud. She was absolutely surreal, showering our executive welcoming team with gratitude and observing how beautiful the landing was in our airport. She was just a gem.

"So fresh and green; and so many lakes!" she cooed in her trademark sultry voice. It was obvious to all of us who met her that despite her top-level celebrity status she was still very down to earth and would be delightful to host. Once settled into her room, I was happy to report back to the group's meeting planner that "the dove", her internal code name, "had landed and was tucked into her nest."

All was good, that is until "the eagle", aka Mr. Rooney, arrived accompanied by his lovely wife and adult son, Mark, whom we affectionately dubbed "Mr. Soul Patch" due to the small patch of beard hair right under his chin (like the ones popularized by really cool jazz musicians and sexy Johnny Depp types, although this one did not look quite that dashing...). As was customary with all our VVIP check ins, we escorted them up to their two-bedroom suite and waited as they entered and inspected everything. Here's where some interesting conversation picked up:

MR. R: This room is quite nice, but I need another shower mat.

HOTEL: No problem, sir. Anything else?

MR. R: Yes. Could you please have housekeeping send up some Preparation H right away?

Luckily, before we could even stifle our smiles, his son chimed in with, "I'll take care of that, dad." Then Mark turned to me and requested a quick private discussion in the hallway.

MARK: Don't you have any other rooms in the hotel available?

ME: Yes of course, is something wrong?

MARK: Please don't make me stay right beside my parents, anywhere else would be fine. Please???

ME: (trying to remain calm and avoid asking the obvious questions like, um, why the heck didn't you provide this information to us earlier?) Okay then, give me a few minutes and let me see what else we can pull out of inventory for you! My Apology, but we just assumed you'd want to stay connected with them in the room next door and...

MARK: Never! I mean, we all live together and well, things can get a little crazy with the two of them and, um, please. Please just move me.

Always wanting to accommodate our guests and keep them happy, we quickly offered another room on the far end of the same floor. We also made dinner reservations for the Rooney family in our wonderful Italian Steakhouse that night. After the room change had been completed and all other details taken care of, Mark assured me they were fine for the evening and I should feel free to go home. No further baby-sitting or hand-holding required. Before I left the hotel, I reported all this back to the main planner telling her "the eagle has landed, is in his nest, and evening feeding arrangements confirmed."

Knowing that I had a few errands to run on the way home, I was a bit anxious to leave. But honestly, as I left the property, I felt confident that everything was in good shape with my group. That is, until my phone rang while I was at my first stop in a store picking up school supplies for my kids.

ME: Hi, this is Sue. What's up?

HOTEL FRONT DESK: Mr. Rooney was just at the desk...

ME: And what does he need?

HOTEL: (uncomfortable hesitation) Um, shorts?

ME: I'm sorry, what…did you just say, shorts?

HOTEL: Yes?

ME: Oh. Was he any more specific?

HOTEL: Well, I kinda think he needs like, you know, men's underwear? Maybe some boxer shorts? (Muffled laugh)

ME: Oh boy. Awesome! (Remembering his earlier spunky request for Preparation H and now this, I couldn't help but chuckle.) Okay then, he's supposed to be dining with his family right now. Could you please transfer me to the steakhouse?

HOTEL: My pleasure! She says while suppressing another muted laugh. (The fun never ends here…)

RESTAURANT RECEPTION: Hi. . . oh yes, hi Sue!

ME: Is Mr. Rooney seated there with his family?

RR: Yes, well he was. Then he just left for a bit, but now he's back.

ME: Do me a favor, please, and go see if his son, Mark, he's the guy sporting a "soul patch", would come from the table and speak with me on this phone line for a quick minute?

RR: Anything I can help you with, Sue?

ME: Thanks, it's a bit of a touchy subject and I think I need to handle this one myself (although in my head I would have loved to pass it off to someone, anyone else…)

MARK: Hi Sue! What's up?

ME: Hi Mark. Well, it seems that, um, well apparently your dad just went to the front desk asking if we could get him some, ah, shorts?

MARK: Shorts?

ME: Yes, as in boxer shorts.

MARK: (Now laughing out loud) Wow-I'm so sorry Sue! What the heck? I can assure you he has plenty of boxers with him! Sorry to have bothered you. I don't know what is going on with him but we're all good here. See you tomorrow.

ME: Well, that's a relief, but thanks, Mark! You know how to reach me if you need to.

RR: (takes phone with not-so-subdued laughter after hearing one end of that conversation) Hi Sue, it's me again. (stifling another chuckle) Just let us know if there is anything else we can help you with, and I mean anything at all! (ha-ha, giggle-giggle)

ME: Yea, we live to serve, right?! Thanks.

The following day is the big gala, and early that morning the planner reviewed all the details with me, stressing about the final timeline. She made it clear that all guests of honor were to be at their designated spots at the convention center promptly at 6PM so I followed that conversation with the car service, reconfirming that the VIP cars with drivers would be waiting in the drive well ahead of that call time. I also learned that the Rooneys were relaxing in their room for most of the day so at that point, all was well.

Until that 2:30PM phone call I received from Mrs. Rooney.

ME: Hi Mrs. Rooney! How are you today?

MRS. R: Fine dear. I just wanted to confirm the dress code for the evening.

ME: I actually received a call earlier today from your planner confirming that the attire is formal ball gown for you and a white dinner jacket tux for Mr. Rooney. Also, just so you know, all the military attendees will be in full uniform, so everyone is sure going to be looking sharp! Oh, and we need to get you to the convention center by 6PM sharp.

MRS. R: (long pause) Well then, that changes everything! I was told it would be business casual, so I have nothing appropriately formal with me. (Huge sigh expressing this inconvenience as if it were total news to her!) I guess I'll need to get a dress. Do you think the dress shop in the hotel might have something?

Me: (after a few seconds of silence while I'm mentally thinking about all the resort wear and workout clothes we carry but certainly no evening gowns) Well let me work on some options for you and...

MRS. R: That's wonderful darling. And, if it's not too much trouble, I'd really like something in blue velour. Size 16. Open neckline, please. And oh, (wait for it...) I do love a few rhinestones on my evening gowns.

ME: Um, okay? (While thinking there's no hope in hell!) Let me noodle on this a bit and get back to you as quickly as possible.

I immediately checked the clock and realized we only had three and a half hours before call time for the big event, so I knew this had to be reported back to the planner immediately. I somehow managed to control the bit of panic in my voice as I briefed her but she was more than a bit concerned about this unexpected announcement and the ensuing challenge it presented. I then tried to reach the Rooney's son, Mark, but had to leave a message as his phone went right to voice mail. As a sidenote, I learned later that he had gone to the NASCAR experience for the afternoon and during my not-so-calm call to him he was probably having the time of his life going 180 miles an hour around that test track. Glad someone could enjoy the afternoon!

So, my options were to either find a clothing concierge to bring some gowns to the hotel or we had to get both Mickey and his wife to a high-end shopping option and do it quickly. Our concierge immediately contacted our closest elite department store to get assistance and they started pulling dresses and tuxes, although in my haste to hang up on that call with Mrs. Rooney I forgot to even get a tux size for Mickey. Luckily while we were still getting this "operation need formal wear now" on the fast track, Mrs. Rooney called me again, this time reporting that her husband did indeed have a tux in his suitcase. (In my mind I'm thinking of course he does - he just can't find his boxer shorts!). Anyway, it was quite a relief to know our main celebrity was all set, especially when thinking about all the alterations that would have been necessary to fit a tuxedo to his particular stature. Whew!

Before I could even switch gears back to the great gown search for Mrs. R, Mark called me from the NASCAR track acknowledging my message and asking me to escort his parents down to the front drive as he'd be there in 20 minutes to take them shopping. I was happy to report back to him that we already had those plans in the works but also quite relieved that he was responsible enough to realize he needed to escort them and help expedite this mission.

So, at approximately 3:45PM I escorted Mr. and Mrs. Rooney to their awaiting son and off on that emergency shopping spree they all went. During all of this I was keeping the planner informed and I could tell by her voice that she was already getting concerned that at least half of her guests of honor were going to be late. As we had not yet heard from the other half of the celebrity duo being honored today, Ann Margaret, I took the time to reach out to her and reconfirm her understanding of the instructions. I was not surprised but quite relieved that she came prepared in the formal gown requirement and would most definitely be on time.

Meanwhile, tick-tock. Tick-tock!

It was now 5:15 pm and I just had to call Mark for an update. To my surprise he advised that they were on their way back and would be on the front drive in less than five minutes, so I hurried down to meet them at the hotel entrance. Up he pulls rather casually with the convertible top down, Mark in the driver's seat and his father on the passenger side. But wait. Full stop here. Someone was definitely missing from this group!

ME: Hi Mark, Mr. Rooney. Um, where is Mrs. Rooney?

MARK: Oh, no worries. We left her at the department store because she wanted to get her makeup and hair done too. But they assured us they will have someone from the store bring her back here in time.

ME: (Gulp. Mouth open but nothing coming out.)

MARK: Really Sue, don't worry! To be honest, well, the other thing is that dad and I absolutely LOVE Whataburgers, so we figured since mom was busy at the store, we'd make a quick stop on the way back. You know we still don't have any in California and...

ME: (Hopefully without a look of complete shock and surprise on my face) OK, well that's great news for you guys, but you DO realize you've got to leave here fully dressed in thirty minutes, so perhaps you and your dad would like to hustle up and get changed? Like immediately. Please?

MARK: We got this, Sue! (Was that a wink he just flashed me?) Dad already had his shower and just needs to get into his tux. I will be cleaned up and ready in no time.

ME: B-b-but, what about your mom?

MARK: She'll make it - pinky promise! Oh, and by the way, the Whataburger was fantastic!

ME: Great. Super. Now get a move on!

And as they hurried up to their respective rooms to finally change, I reluctantly phoned the planner - again - to check in and give a progress report on "operation get these celebrities to their awards banquet across the street on time." After a few choice words from her (better not to repeat in print), I promised to update her every blessed remaining step of the way including when I see both Mr. Soul Patch and his crazy-ass dad, plus when I see the whites of the eyes on the driver returning Mrs. Rooney who would very hopefully be well coiffed and ready to show her awesomeness.

Meanwhile, I might also add that the gorgeous Ms. Ann Margaret casually glided down to the entrance looking stunning in her designer gown and taking her time to stop and acknowledge people along the way. She made an effort to greet everyone and could not have been more congenial to her appreciative fans, many of whom were speechless at the surprise appearance of one of television's most iconic beauties.

As for the three-ring-Rooney circus, we were finally able to load Mark along with both his mom and dad into their awaiting limo at only five minutes late, and if I hadn't seen it with my own eyes, I never would have believed it!

But I gotta tell you that every time I pass by that Whataburger, I can't help but think of Mickey Rooney and his boxer shorts and Mrs. Rooney's search for an incredibly specific evening gown at the very last minute!

Lessons Learned:

- ✓ When dealing with celebrities, take nothing for granted. You cannot assume anything, as the saying goes, "the devil is in the details."
- ✓ A best practice would always be to provide a written timeline to VIPs so as to avoid any miscommunications between their handlers and everyone else surrounding their entourage.

SUE KING BIO: After thirty-seven years in the hotel industry working for the largest convention center in the US and some of the top convention hotels in Orlando, Dallas and New York, Sue has now established herself as an independent planner specializing in trade show and food service management. She likes to say she is "standing in the hole" because with a background this strong in hospitality, there is basically nothing in the realm of meetings and conventions that she hasn't seen, done, or fixed! Sue has one dog and most importantly two beautiful grandbabies, so even when she's not "officially" working, she really is always working.

https://www.linkedin.com/in/sueking/

CHAPTER THIRTEEN

Events from the Entertainer's Viewpoint

By Karen Kuzsel, aka Natasha the Psychic Lady

EDITOR'S NOTE: Karen has multiple personalities: writer, publisher, speaker, dancer and blogger to name a few– along with being a successful entertainer centered on psychic readings and various other intriguing mystical talents. As an active member of both MPI and ILEA, she has earned her industry credentials by serving on multiple local and national committees over the past twenty plus years. As her alter ego, Natasha the Psychic Lady, Karen has been a featured performer at Walt Disney World and is also frequently seen at all the Central Florida theme parks along with countless major corporations during their conventions and trade shows. The following stories are some of the unique experiences she's encountered when hired to work these events.

In her words:
About being placed in dark corners when I have to read tarot cards. And oh boy, guests behaving badly. . .

Funny and challenging things can happen when client events are pushed ahead, or more routinely, running behind. I cannot tell you the number of times I've been dressed in full makeup and costume, only to be left waiting. Then waiting some more. Not even daring to go to the bathroom for fear the client's guests would finally show up because yes, that happens when the client does not fully communicate or even enforce their own timelines. As both a speaker and entertainer, I never get used to this frustration.

One event stands out because a more actively aware meeting coordinator would have been an asset. That evening was Halloween. The group members were morticians and their families. My designated location was in the farthest corner of the ballroom away from the band. Normally, that would have been a plus because I need to talk to people while reading their palms or tarot. Being close to music blasting provides enough challenges, however, because this was Halloween, the room was severely darkened to create a spooky atmosphere adding to the difficulty in my being seen and heard. The corner I was placed in was dimly lit by slim light creeping in from the hallway. In addition to the darkened location, there had been a miscommunication between the meeting planner and the hotel about the start time of the party. By my contractually scheduled time, the guests showed up one-and-one-half hours late so, of course, the first thing on their minds was to feed their families, not scout the dark room out for entertainment possibilities.

Knowing it would be a while before anyone made their way to my corner, I decided to walk around the dinner tables to introduce myself and assure them of my fun, family-friendly readings. My table was set with an expansive display of tarot cards, runes, crystal ball and candles all on a metaphysical tablecloth so there was much to entice everyone if only they could find me in that dimly lit corner! I should also mention that usually when I leave my table, I cover it with a cloth, but I skipped that step this time because the coordinator was nearby, and her table was chock full of fun party giveaways that I knew she would be monitoring. Plus, I did inform her of my plan to go work the crowd a bit so at least she knew I would be back shortly.

I made the rounds and hurried back to my table, certain that my personal marketing would have plenty of guests flocking my way soon. As I approached my dark corner, I already saw a family seated all around my table and thought, "Great, my greetings worked and they're waiting for me!" That is, until I got close enough to see that they had pushed my precious props aside and set all their food plates and drinks down on my obviously ornamental tablecloth to enjoy their meal. This was so inappropriate on many levels!

And this is also where things get tricky for an entertainer. I would have preferred that the coordinator assist with this problem, but of course she was missing in action, so I had to handle this myself. I carefully explained to the family that this was my worktable (which should have been obvious) and I was sorry, but they would need to find somewhere else to eat. One of the kids, who by now was playing with my real crystal ball (not an inexpensive object), looked up and asked what was going on. The father replied angrily, "This lady is making us leave."

Silently I thought, "Did they not realize that 'this lady' was all decked out in a flashy, mystical costume and glitter makeup to entertain them at this table? Or that the expensive crystal ball your son thinks is a toy shouldn't be touched?"

But of course, I kept that to myself.

Then I watched as they indignantly picked up their drinks and stormed off, but not without leaving me a 'tip'. Yep, that entire family left their dirty dishes on my table!

"What????"

Now I was in a situation where I feared they might go complain to the party host saying that I had upset them, of course omitting that they had invaded my space. Not a good start for my evening of entertainment!

Also, this was not the first time I have had event guests leaving their "stuff" on my table, not by a long shot. I have lost track of how often I'll be intently reading someone's palm, tarot, runes or energy and people will walk by and casually drop their drink glasses, plates, dirty napkins onto my table leaving me to bus it myself back to the kitchen or to a nearby tray jack. In those instances, I'm unsure who is more taken aback at the rude interruption: the guest I'm engaged in reading or me. That's one of the many reasons I do prefer strolling the room while mingling with guests, but occasionally I am seated by client request.

Next up, what was the planner thinking?

Five things planners do that complicate my level of performance service:

1. Ask me to read tarot cards when the wind is gusting or it's raining at an outdoor event and no protection is provided.
2. Ask me to read palms in a pitch-black room ("for the atmosphere") or under a moonless night outside. Granted, I always have battery-candles which emit a low light and I always have a magnifying light, but that means the guest cannot see what I am trying to describe as I point to specific lines and bumps on their palm, an important aspect of being a palm reader.

3. Position me beside an amplifier. Who would have thought that a psychic would need to be heard while dispensing witty insights or that trying to talk over intense music might be a strain of my vocal cords, let alone be a barrier to what can be heard? Over the many years of working events and having this happen repeatedly, I try to gracefully explain that me shouting into someone's ear is probably not the great guest experience they are hoping to achieve and perhaps I could be moved from the direct blast of sound? I wish I could say that common sense plea always works, sigh, but...

4. Do not put my table beside an open-flame heater lamp on a windy night. Yes, this has happened more than a few times, but the worst was a hotel lawn event. The flames were flickering as if trying to lick me each time the wind gusted. After it got dangerously close to the guest and me, I finally had to stop the reading and seek help. It should not have been my job to figure out those type of heat lamps and wind were not a compatible mix.

5. Don't put my table beside cigar rollers and smokers. I have allergies. I literally get nauseous and get horrid sinus headaches. Not a good combination when you are hired to entertain. I am happy to stroll in areas (far away) with minimal direct contact with those smokers, but if you are the planner, please understand that not all elements of your themed event are compatible.

6. Not provide a correct location name and address for the gig. Many entertainers must schlep plenty of equipment with us from our parking locations, and let's just say it's no fun when we appear in full costume pulling/ pushing said paraphernalia only to discover we are in the wrong venue!

More fun times. Mardi Gras? What Mardi Gras?

This is about that time when I was told explicitly to dress flamboyantly for a Mardi Gras themed event and that the guests would also be decked out. You say flamboyant and hey, I'm an entertainer, so I bring out the beads and feathers on top of my green gold, and purple flashy finest!

Unfortunately, when I walked in the room, I quickly discovered two things: 1) There were no decorations at all. None. Nada. 2) Guests were all in casual clothing. Ooops!

The stares were priceless. I gulped once, and then walked in boldly and amusedly declared, "What, you didn't get the costume memo?"

The lessons I've learned (the hard and embarrassing way) is to check, double-check and then reconfirm all details such as theme, color scheme, type of readings they want me to conduct, age of group, indoor/outdoor locations, correct address (RE to #6 above because yes, it has happened more than once that I've been sent to a wrong address!). These might all seem like standard details but again, I speak from the voice of experience by mentioning all this and more.

That time when none of the guests spoke English!

This was a gem because the client had asked not only for me but for two additional psychics to work a large international group. There were multiple parties in all the hotel ballrooms, and the three of us were spread out and ready to entertain. Until realizing we couldn't.

Seems a tiny bit of extremely important information had not been communicated. All the guests were Japanese and spoke no English making reading their palms, our tarot cards or basically anything an impossible task.

Then there were the tax lawyers. . .

My booking agent had carefully described my services to the client as reading by touch, meaning that I put my hands on their wrists and sensed their energy. Sometimes I "hear" words or "see" pictures in my head and describe that for my reading. Two things went horribly wrong at this event:

1. Onsite, the association's planners freaked out that I would touch the men, who represented about 98% of those in attendance. Even though that was the service that was sold to them, I had to swiftly switch gears. Crises averted, but what if reading by touch were my only talent and I had nothing else to offer the client that night?

2. The second malfunction was the band. I have no idea or explanation why, but the planners hired an excessively loud heavy metal kick-ass rock & roll band. On the plus side they would have been awesome to dance to, but remember when I mentioned above the audience was 98% male? Yeah, there was that. No one braved the dance floor (shocking, right?), plus the music was so loud the attendees couldn't network, causing many of them to leave early.

To conclude, I have certainly experienced plenty of mayhem at meetings over the course of my career as an entertainer. This was just a snapshot of some of the more unique situations I've encountered, all in a day's work for this gal.

KAREN KUZSEL BIO: What do you get when you mix a woman of Polish, Romanian, Hungarian and Austrian heritage (whose numerous relatives routinely read tea leaves, tarot cards and were telepathic) with a gypsy-styled dancer, and who also has a solid background as an entertainment Writer-Editor-and Publisher? You get Natasha, the Psychic Lady, whose own modalities of "tuning in" include energy, psychometry, palmistry, handwriting analysis, tarot cards, lip reading, runes, tea leaves, and coffee grounds. Describing herself as "the plastic surgeon of the Psychic set" because she only wants to deal with the beautiful (of spirit and all things positive), Natasha is a frequent speaker for corporate and organizational meetings. She maintains a blog focusing on hotel happenings, destinations, and events all around the world and another where she shares recipes straight from her test kitchen.

www.Karenkuzsel.com

http://www.thepsychiclady.com/

CHAPTER FOURTEEN

Australian Air Show Sizzler

By Michael D. Lynn, CEM, CME, CMM,
CMP, CPC, CPECP

It was the Sizzler to remember at one of the first **Australian International Air Shows***. As was customary for participating exhibitors in these massive productions held semi-annually in and around major transnational airports, we had spent several weeks in pre-production building out both my company's exhibit and the **chalet*** (similar to the hospitality tents you see at major sporting events) to our incredibly detailed specs for that event. During the show we would be hosting brunches, lunches, and plenty of cocktail receptions for our anticipated high-level clients (think top brass military from major and minor worldwide countries along with scattered celebrities and corporate titans who buy or fly their own aircraft).

Now this show was held in February which in Australia is smack in the middle of summer, and that year they were experiencing a unique heat wave. It was so intense I actually lost about twelve pounds just from the constant work needed to get things done on time, and remember we were working in and around an active airport runway, so the heat was even more intensified, by some estimates as high as 115 degrees! Plus, weather predictions were anticipating that it was still going to be a scorcher during the actual trade show days still ahead of us. Oh boy.

At most of these international air shows the exhibition halls and chalets are usually provided with normal air conditioning units, but as this was their first Australian air show plus the soaring temperatures were exceptionally off the charts this year, adequate A/C units had not been factored into the necessary equipment orders. Instead, the show organizers used what is called a swamp cooler which is the normal Aussie answer to a portable A/C unit but is basically just air being blown over a radiator type filter while running regular tap water through it. We quickly discovered this lowers the temp only about a solid eight degrees, and when it is already blazing hot outside, you know what it's going to be like trying to comfortably entertain and impress high caliber guests in your fancy chalet and gigantic exhibit. We knew there was trouble up ahead.

So, we started checking all avenues on trying to find better A/C options, especially for that all-important Chalet, including local and international hardware supply companies, plumbing contractors, even the airport itself. You think of a place and either I or the local man in charge of my event buildout, Alan, probably called them. Plus, the clock was now ticking to the arrival of our corporate senior staff who we knew positively would not be pleased with the prospect of attempting to conduct multi-million-dollar pieces of business in a sweat box.

But while still profusely perspiring at the event site on the final morning of pre-show prep (meaning it was down to the wire with that heating and cooling problem and, also just as importantly, D-Day for me and my career), Alan pulls up and tells me to jump in his van. Off we went to Geelong, a port city southwest of Melbourne, and about an hour later we pulled up in front of a private home and hopped out. As we entered the yard, Alan introduced me to his brother and explained we were there to "borrow some things." While his brother and other helpers were occupied loading a few miscellaneous items into the van, we actually snatched his brother's A/C units right from the windows of his home! Then we high tailed it out of there as fast as we could, but not without getting an earful of shouting between the Aussie brothers.

"Hey mate! What 'em I goin' to tell the Mrs.?"

"No worries, mate! I'll 'av 'em back to you within a week!"

As you can well imagine in the end, this made our Chalet a huge hit and everyone at the show wanted to stop by and "take a meeting" (meaning cool off) with our team of happy executives. We were, in fact, the most popular chalet at the show, no small accomplishment for a show of this size and magnitude!

As a side note, two years later when the air show returned to Australia, we again contracted with Alan who this time had the foresight to plan ahead for another expected heat wave ordering four large commercial A/C units since, due to our past popularity at this show, we also had a larger chalet. Go figure! But apparently, we were a bit overzealous in our planning to need four units of that strength as we discovered the first time we powered up and watched their awesome energy blast out the false ceiling panels of that temporary chalet roof! On the positive side we also had an instantly cool outdoor patio area, too.

Plus, at future shows the event organizer did finally start providing better air conditioning options for all the exhibit halls and chalets. But just to be safe, most US companies still provide their own.

*International Air Shows: Held globally at airport locations in places such as Paris, Asia, and Australia, these are like other industry trade shows except for the size and amount of money that is spent in order to showcase products of this magnitude and scope. Exhibit displays include wide-body commercial aircraft, helicopters, defense products and all the components involved in the manufacture of such simple items as seat cushions and carpeting but also including technical cockpit equipment and missile systems. It is not uncommon for a manufacturer of this type of product to spend multi millions of dollars in order to showcase their goods, and as the name indicates, there is always an actual air show component showcasing sophisticated landing, takeoff and flight exhibitions.

*Exhibition Halls and Chalets: Again, similar to other industry trades shows except that these facilities are built to showcase products of massive size and are therefore done in close proximity to where the aircraft can land meaning near flight lines and large capacity runways. Chalets are used for sophisticated corporate hospitality during the air show and attendees are comprised of the highest-ranking military officials from all over the world, corporate officers from among global industry titans, and of course, various sports and other celebrities in the market for purchasing their own aircraft. As with the air show itself, millions of dollars are spent wining and dining potential customers of these multimillion dollar purchases.

Lessons Learned:

✓ Planning is the backbone of success.
✓ Never assume something is included in your price unless it is outlined in your contract or event specs.

No detail is too small, or in this case too large, to 'make an assumption' about it being included.

✓ Necessity creates opportunities

MICHAEL LYNN BIO: Michael graduated with Dual Masters from Embry-Riddle Aeronautical University and began a distinguished 21-year career with the US Air Force, ten of which were highlighted flying both Air Force One (transporting the US President) and Air Force Two (carrying the Vice President) on their global travels. After military retirement, he became Director of Events & Protocol to the aeronautical defense industry and was selected as a consultant to the movie, "Air Force One" starring Harrison Ford. Today he is one of the founding partners of the Global Protocol, Etiquette, Civility, Academy based in Dallas, TX, and spends his time as a speaker/trainer on security issues and global protocol. If you noticed all those credentials behind his name, they are for real as Michael is known professionally as "The Ambassador of Certifications" maintaining credentials in multiple international organizations.

http://www.globalpecacademy.com/

CHAPTER FIFTEEN

The Moonstone Marble Tablecloths

By Terry Matthews-Lombardo, CMP

The ballroom looked gorgeous. Three hundred banquet tables, all 72" rounds set with a wonderfully comfortable eight chairs per table (instead of cramming in ten to twelve seats as is often done), set in an alternating pattern so that when guests entered the room they would view an impressive and dramatic diagonal arrangement instead of straight lines leading to the stage. A small detail to some, but as all meeting planners know, can be that one detail that makes your room set look spectacular as opposed to 'meh.' This is because if you do not specify exact placement of tables and chairs in your diagram of the room set, the venue will always just assume you want everything in boring but standard straight lines, and it will look average at best.

And speaking of straight lines, this is where my story takes a turn in the wrong direction, pun intended. You see, each of those three hundred tables had a lovely, luxurious floor length tablecloth on it in a pattern, called "moonstone marble", specifically chosen by my client for its' dreamy, wavy, artsy-fartsy illusion. But apparently that "marble illusion" was not exactly providing the symmetric site line that my client had hoped for once she saw all three hundred of them set in the ballroom.

I believe her exact words were, and I quote, "EGADS! We CAN'T. HAVE. THIS!"

And just like that she decided that if "we" (meaning me) were to "just" turn the cloths around (meaning remove the 132" floor length tablecloths from each one of the three hundred tables) and place it in a different direction "LIKE THIS", THEN they would be perfectly aligned with the diagonal direction of the table scape and ambience that she was going for.

Yeah, right.

Why didn't I think of that before? Better yet, why didn't the blasted rental company from which she had rented all those expensive linens think of that before they dropped them on each and every table, all positioned in the wrong freakin' direction?

And if this sounds like a head scratcher to you as in "does anybody really pay any attention to that sort of thing when they walk into a ballroom?" then you would be a very normal person. You would also be opposite of my client because she proceeded to insist–no, I should say INSIST, because she only spoke in capital letters–on me turning all those tablecloths into a more "perfect" position.

All righty then, let's turn these tablecloths!

But this is the part where I need to mention I was currently working solo in the ballroom as the linen rental company had left the minute all the cloths were dropped (did I mention incorrectly, at least in my client's eyes?) and the rest of my staff was busy setting up registration and handling other areas that still needed attention. Plus, *the great tablecloth caper* now needed to be done before the flower arrangements were dropped in the center of each table, which needed to be done before the hotel service staff walked in wheeling miles of carts full of table settings that needed to be *perfectly and systematically* placed (think cutlery, multiple plates and glasses X eight people per table, napkins, bread baskets, salt & pepper shakers, butter dishes, etc.). We even had a crew of wait staff who's only job was to fold napkins "just so" for this gorgeous table setting, and they were already busy in a back-of-house area focusing on their own extremely specific assignment.

Sooooo, off I go to table #1 or as I like to say, ground zero, because at this point we hadn't even put the table numbers on yet, and trust me on this point, you really have to pay attention to where you start and proceed so you're not wasting time back tracking and possibly repositioning a tablecloth that you've already "turned" because you've seriously just lost your mind and agreed to do this so now anything is possible! The voice in your head has confirmed that you really and truly are working in a looney bin for an in-sane client, and this is the absolute stupidest waste of time you have ever agreed to. But what the heck.

And I know you're wondering, "how hard can this task be?"

Glad you asked because it was at ground zero that I also discovered just how heavy those marvelous mother-lovin' moonstone marble tablecloths were. Would you believe they each weighed almost five pounds? And did I mention there were three hundred tables with a top spread of 72"? *And that I was working alone?* And, well, tick-tock. **Tick-tock!**

Yeah, then there was that. I basically had less than an hour to get all these tables in order and needless to say it was not nearly enough time for one person to accomplish this task. I quickly enlisted any and everybody I could finagle, sweet talk and yes, bribe (thank you sweet off duty AV guys who will do anything for the promise of some food later on) to take a row and get to work, post haste. *Chop-chop!* The "Inspector

General" would be showing up again soon and well, you just know she would be looking at each and every tablecloth, and I fully expected she'd be returning with a yardstick to measure everything and check those site lines.

So, exactly how long does it take to turn around three hundred marble moonstone tablecloths to make them all perfectly pointed in a symmetrically directional pattern as specified by your client?

Too. Long. Way, way too long.

Lesson Learned:

✓ NO DETAIL–even the direction of the pattern on your tablecloths (!)–should be left to guesswork. During the day-of setup process, there should always be a fully set sample table with all the "bells and whistles" (dishes, napkins, florals, printed menus, etc.) on display for client's approval so that all parties involved can refer to that as they commence to complete the rest of the table sets.

As the creator and overall author of this book, my brief bio can be found on the back cover. And if you enjoy my writing style, please consider subscribing to my infrequently posted travel and industry blogs (hey, I'm also a working meeting planner!) that you can find here:

www.terrysworldtravels.com

Chapter Sixteen

Before There Was COVID, Legionnaire's Disease Found a Way into My Meeting!

As told to tml by Wendy Porter, Chief Event Architect,
Wendy Porter Events, LLC

EDITOR'S NOTE: As I write this (mid 2020) the number one thing on everyone's mind around the world is the Coronavirus that has pretty much brought this planet to a standstill for an undetermined time frame, but we all know that there have been other deadly diseases in the past that also rocked the universe in different ways. This story is about one of them, Legionnaire's Disease, that has a history of "checking in" to hotels, and well, we all know there's really no good time to have a deadly disease check in to your hotel, right?

SCENE SET: It is 2012 and Wendy, our veteran meeting planner, has just arrived at a four-star property in Chicago to manage a weeklong program for her company involving just under one thousand attendees arriving equally distributed in two different **back-to-back waves.** * This constituted a total **hotel buy out*** which means it's a pretty big piece of business in both financial terms and in client stature. It's also a *heckofalotof* work for a meeting planner including being on call 24/7 while on site with the program, so also not a great time to get sick. Or to contract a deadly disease. Or to find out that some of your attendees are ill after having contracted said disease during the program your company is sponsoring. Yeah, that's what this story is about…

WENDY SPEAKS: The first few days that week were fine, just the normal work-work-work to get things ready for the day one major arrivals. I wasn't feeling anything unusual other than stress and pressure, which for meeting planners is well, not at all unusual! It's what fuels us forward. But after powering through the first couple of days I suddenly woke up·queasy, and not in a "I had too much to drink last night" way but the real deal. Fever. Aches and pains. Wheezing. And eventually all the rest of the *lucky motherlode* of being sick manifests itself and you Just. Don't. Care.

TML: But you were still trying to work through it, right? I mean, how did that go for you?

WENDY: Well, there came a point when a colleague just said NO–you have got to stay in bed! I hunkered down in my hotel room, and did I mention they had placed me in the luxurious, expansive Presidential Suite for that week? I was so sick I didn't even care or appreciate those posh surroundings.

TML: And at that point did you have any idea that some of the other attendees were also sick?

WENDY: Listen, I was so sick I wouldn't have particularly cared if there was a 300-piece marching band parading through that Presidential Suite, but to answer your question, no, not really. This *"thing"* did not yet have a name, was spreading slowly so people were just individually isolating and not necessarily bombarding the hotel (yet) with reports of their sickness. Remember, this was years before COVID 19 hit the planet and

real time reaction was not playing out in front of a large inter-
active social media audience. If you were sick you stayed in bed.

TML: Got it. But then what happened?

WENDY: Well, exactly eight days after I arrived in Chicago, I gave up the good fight in that plush hotel room and
attempted to fly home.

TML: And...?

WENDY: Well, here is where the story takes another turn.
I get into the limousine the company had arranged to take me
to the airport, but I didn't really make it much farther than a
block or so before, um...

TML: Mt. Etna blew again?

WENDY: (Gives a rather embarrassed positive nod in
response.)

TML: Yikes! In the limo?

WENDY: Yep. Let's just say it wasn't my finest transport
and move on with the story. But for purposes of full disclosure, I did darn sure make amends and take care of that limo
driver after he carefully returned me to the lobby and before
he departed the hotel! So, moving on, my colleague attempted
to check me right back into the room I had just vacated only
to find it was no longer available (not that I cared where I was
going to die, I just wanted to be comfortable on that final journey). So eventually, I settled into a different room for about
four more days after which time I did finally make it home
where I continued to hunker down until fully recovered.

But, before we get to that happy ending, fast forward a few
more days to when I got a call from HR. We now had over 30
people reporting being sick and they confirmed it was Legionnaires. I promptly called my local clinic to get in for a test and
was prescribed a 21 day course of a "big gun" antibiotic, and as
I recall it was something akin to a horse pill. Believe it or not,

I actually had the frame of mind to read the instructions and almost fainted when I saw "sometimes used to treat the black plague and anthrax exposure" but heck, I took it anyway. What choice did I have?

BACKSTORY CONCLUSION: Wendy continued to take the prescribed medicine for the next three weeks. But once an investigation was launched and all the data had been gathered, this group counted about 90 confirmed cases of illness, some with Legionnaire's and others with the less serious form of the disease called Pontiac Fever. Several from the group ended up in intensive care and *one colleague tragically passed away*. All told, **the exposure led to at least five dead from people staying on the property during that time of exposure. Yes, dead.** Wendy herself says it took a solid three months of coughing and suffering through respiratory sickness before she really felt any level of health again.

As for the hotel, what was their reaction and response to this outbreak? First, they discovered that the primary source of the infection was found in the **Legionella bacteria*** that had spawned in the hotel's decorative fountain located right there in the main lobby, obviously a popular spot for all hotel guests to pass by daily. Wendy herself had spent quite a substantial amount of time at that fountain, aka "ground zero", one night as she provided meet-and-greet services for all her attendees before sending them off to their respective dine-around locations, so they were confident that this is where her exposure had been. This strain of bacteria grows in warm water temperatures and is transmitted as the water vaporizes, floating around in the air on those water droplets circulating from the fountain. Standing anywhere near that source well, voila. It is easily inhaled and ultimately becomes a severe form of bacterial pneumonia.

The good news was that because it is a bacterial infection, it is not a contagious disease nor is it transmitted from person-to-person human contact. The bad news was that plenty of hotel guests (by some estimates as many as 8500) were affected before it was discovered and eradicated from the water source. Wendy confirmed that there were indeed inevitable lawsuits following this discovery but she, herself, was not part of that legal action.

EDITOR'S FINAL NOTE: As a reminder, this story took place long before Coronavirus in 2020, so even though we are all now quite used to hearing warnings about the transmission of bacteria via water droplets and the importance of wearing face masks to prevent the spread, those had never before become "a thing" in our daily lives.

*__back-to-back waves__: when the sum total or multiple segments of a meeting or convention is split into two or more sectors, each running start-to-finish right up until the beginning of the next one, thus 'the wave' caused by attendees at check in, check out.

*__hotel buyout__: a meeting of substantial size that essentially buys all the meeting space and sleeping rooms in a particular hotel in order to accommodate their group needs for a specified period of time.

*__Legionella bacteria__: can cause a serious, sometimes fatal, type of pneumonia (lung infection) called Legionnaires' disease. The bacteria can also cause a less serious mild flu-like illness called Pontiac fever.

Lessons Learned:

✓ Your inquiry into sanitation methods and protocols in your event venue should include many details you've never even thought of such as those needed for public water features/fountains and pool/spa areas since, as in our case, these areas were ground zero for the spread of this deadly virus.

✓ Check your contracts to ensure there is insurance coverage by the property for illness/disease exposure, and always seek legal counsel to assure the proper wording is in place to secure this.

WENDY PORTER BIO: Wendy is a veteran planner who worked for many years in marketing and events for some major US corporations before founding her own meetings and events company, Wendy Porter Events. Based in Minneapolis, WPE specializes in both live and virtual events, meetings, and galas. She has won numerous industry accolades and honors, and when she's not traveling the world for business or pleasure, you'll find her speaking (in German!) to the plants in her award-winning garden or loving on her Australian Shepherd.

www.wendyporterevents.com

CHAPTER SEVENTEEN

"Fun" with Celebrities

By Connie Riley, CMP, CSEP Emeritus

Before there were cellphones. . .

In 1996 we were managing a corporate show and the headline act was Martina McBride who had just won the coveted Country Music Association's Video of the Year award for her hit single, Independence Day. Although we had booked her prior to even receiving the nomination, by the time our event happened she had won and was on top of her game, so showing up for a standard corporate performance was not a big effort for a "hot commodity" celebrity. Unbeknownst to me or anyone else working the show that day, Martina, who did not yet even have her own personal assistant, decided to go out shopping in the limo provided for her. This would not normally have been an issue, but cell phones were not even a thing yet so none of us had communication with her or the driver which of course wasn't discovered until just a curtain call away from show time. Now, whether she lost track of time or really wasn't at all worried about this engagement we will never know but all I remember is the panic backstage when everyone was still frantically searching for our star performer even moments before she successfully and gracefully stepped on stage – while still applying her makeup! But to her credit she was right on cue to take the spotlight.

Lessons Learned:

✓ Always control the transportation and, of course now that we all use cell phones, exchange numbers with your driver.

✓ Give specific instructions to your driver to let you know all trips and requests made by their passengers (your clients) in order to keep tabs on their location. This should include a detailed timeline so that everyone understands both call and show times.

Before there were cellphones, part two:

This show was on the top floor pavilion of the San Diego Convention Center, and Marilyn McCoo was performing on the closing night of a corporate client's convention. Leading up to the show, everything went as planned. The convention center staff was prepared and the arrival, load in, catering, sound check all went as scheduled. The pavilion was an upstairs covered deck with the dressing rooms several floors beneath using elevators for access. Just prior to showtime, our account exec went downstairs to escort Marilyn from the dressing rooms only to discover that all the elevators were only going one way and unfortunately that was all the way down to the loading dock! This was specifically done as a temporary security feature to prevent unauthorized guests from accessing our group's private event space after hours. Well back when this happened in 1998 there were no cell phones, so the account exec made a frantic search of the loading dock finally making contact with a lonely security officer about to get the thrill of his life while figuring out how to deliver this celebrity to her top deck destination, pronto! Show time was moments away and Marilyn was beginning to show signs of stress between the long-distance walking on that loading dock and not knowing how this evening would end. Eventually, security secured a functioning elevator going to the top and she was able to deliver another flawless performance despite the last-minute stress and unexpected entrance.

Lesson Learned:

✓ When escorting celebrities, speakers, or any high-level executives to a backstage location, insist to meet with security ahead of time to review your plans, and then actually take that walk together.
✓ Thoroughly review a timeline for getting this task done, exchange phone numbers and identify contacts for emergencies along with emergency procedures.

Cell phones? Yes. Dali Lama? No!

BLACK EYED PEAS - 2005

We contracted the Black Eyed Peas for Quicken Loans in Cleveland, 2005, for the name change from the Gund Arena to Quicken Loans Arena. This was to be a family event with games for the children on the upper concourse along with the food concessions and plenty of buffet stations set throughout the venue. One year prior the Black Eyed Peas had released "Let's Get It Started" (a reworked version of "Let's Get Retarded") for the 2004 NBA Playoffs so they were hitting a high note in their career.

Despite that, the show was a comedy of errors. Will.i.am had been told by his agent that he would meet the Dalai Lama if he accepted the gig. (?) At one point he asked my team member when he was going to meet the Dalai Lama and after receiving a blank look, the Road Manager told him the truth.

Then there was Fergie who decided to take an afternoon dance class. She did make it back in time for the show but forgot her costumes and make up at the hotel. We had to send a van back for her items, but then that van broke down in the valet driveway at the hotel and had to be towed to a repair shop! Lucky for us her manager had no sympathy and sent her on stage in her rehearsal outfit including whatever make up she and her assistant had on hand.

But the funniest challenge happened between sound check and show.

The Quicken Loans Arena is right next-door to the Cleveland Indians baseball park. On game days the Cleveland police close the streets to control traffic. While we knew there was a scheduled game the day of our show, we had not understood that the police would string caution tape across all streets that accessed our loading dock next door at the Quicken Loans Arena. I was leading the caravan of band member vehicles to the arena and fortunately had practiced this drive several times over two days, so I knew the route. But of course, my run throughs had not encountered any roadblocks or yellow caution tape! I quickly jumped out of the van looking for assistance from the police, but none were in sight. With the clock ticking to show time, I decided to take my chances and lift that yellow caution tape as high over my head as I could while motioning to all the vehicles to keep driving right under the tape and continue the journey. You can imagine my relief when all of those vehicles holding the entire group of Black Eyed Peas musicians finally completed the last leg down the driveway under the arena and delivered to their designated location, on schedule. Whew! At last we had the band in the arena and standing by in our holding area, the Cleveland Cavaliers Locker Room. But guess who else was there? All the Cavalier basketball players!

And still, the best part of this story is yet to come!

We all knew the Black Eyed Peas used foul language so in all negotiations for this private performance for a corporate client they had contractually agreed to keep their lyrics family friendly and their dancing wholesome. But when I went back -with police escort - to walk the band out to the stage, what I did not anticipate was what I found after I knocked on that busy locker room door, now filled with all my musicians AND the entire team of Cleveland Cavs.

Both doors fly open, and a huge billowing white cloud of funny smelling smoke greets us at the door. Not kidding! It took a minute for the smoke to clear before the band and players appeared during which time all I could think of is, "we're doomed!" I'm in a Cheech and Chong movie and the Black Eyed Peas are hosting the marijuana smoke-in for the Cleveland Cavaliers basketball players. And we are all going to jail!

Well, guess what? No arrests, no comments from the police or the NBA, and the Black Eyed Peas were true to their word. No foul language plus a great show.

Never mind that my nerves were shot!

Lessons Learned:

✓ Even with permits and private venues, if you are in a public area, share your plans with the local police departments.

✓ I'm sure there was another lesson about the whole marijuana deal, but once I knew the police were turning a blind eye, I just counted my blessings and kept repeating to myself, "the show must go on!"

AUTHOR'S NOTE: One common thread in all the above stories, and in fact, any event I've worked during my career that has encountered a glitch, is that a lack of communication between all parties involved usually leads to some surprises, and that usually leads to trouble. I can't stress enough the importance of holding all-inclusive tie down meetings prior to any event so that all parties involved are working off the same timeline and can compare everyone's priorities on one shared checklist.

CHAPTER EIGHTEEN

James Brown Blows a Fuse

Also by Connie Riley, CMP. CSEP Emeritus

Soul music prevailed in the DC suburbs where I grew up in the late 1960's. I spent countless hours dancing, memorizing lyrics and falling in love with many soul artists so you can imagine, in my current life as a show producer, how excited I get when I find myself working with numerous of those iconic celebrity soul artists. Sometimes it's loads of fun; except when it's not. This is that story.

For many years, we produced a celebrity concert in the summer for a closing night event at the end of a client's conference. Attendance was usually around 1000-1500, and the event was actually held outside in the expansive Porte Cochere area of the host hotel. Because of our successful multi-year history with this client, we had a reliable production partner and lots of musicians willing to assist as both stagehands and runners. This was necessary due to the considerable distance from loading dock to outdoor staging to dressing rooms to the meet-and- greet locations, so our extra-large team was kept busy. And in this case, some of them even worked in exchange for the opportunity to stay and enjoy the concert which is not always possible but in this case was a very desirable option considering our featured act was the Godfather of Soul himself, James Brown.

But each year before the star act steps on stage, this client always used the same wildly popular audience-pleasing cover band brought in from Atlanta, and they always had one caveat in their contract stating a requirement to strike their own band's equipment immediately following their set. This practice is not usually suggested during a live performance but because that cover band contracted directly with the client, the issue was out of our control as we had been contracted only to manage the stage production and star performer. And if there is one thing I have learned for sure during all my years in this industry is that when contractual issues are "out of our control" well, trouble is sure to follow. Let me explain the specifics.

Any changeover between performance groups needs to be done quickly and efficiently to keep the event flowing smoothly, on schedule, and most importantly to keep the crowd engaged as they anxiously await the star billing celebrity act.

So, back to when the trouble began.

Set up day went as planned. Installation began at dawn with load in of the stage, sound, and lighting. Bus parking, limousines containing the celebrity and his band arrived, dressing rooms, catering and security were managed, and sound checks ran as intended. So far, the day was on schedule for all parties involved.

The event began on time, the cover act performed and as always, got the crowd excited and ready for what was to come. Once they ended, we immediately switched to pre-selected recorded music played over the extensive sound system to keep the audience pumped as we commenced the dreaded changeover.

At this point it was all hands on deck as my crew struck the cover band's equipment and the very particular James Brown backstage team worked alongside my stagehands to get the job done. Switches were checked, expensive guitars were brought out of insured traveling storage cases and delicately placed in their respective stands, microphones were tested for volume and monitors aimed accordingly. So far so good.

While both crews worked in tandem on stage, I was backstage managing the star. This required that I take a flight of stairs downstairs to the dressing rooms located inside the hotel to wrangle the Godfather of Soul and his band plus a full security entourage. Nothing unusual until you are in the thick of things as of course, the energy flow is heightened, and the stress meter can climb to the roof in a split second. On this evening once we were upstairs, I swear I only left James Brown and his Manager in the wings for a New York minute so that I could assure all was well once our celebrity took to the stage. In that time, I could clearly see the cover band's equipment had been removed and was still being loaded onto their awaiting bus, plus the JB crew was still tweaking things to the star and band's exact specification.

Great. We were still on schedule.

Until we weren't, because it happens just that fast!

While I proudly stood cued up backstage right next to "the man", suddenly there was a loud buzzing and popping through the sound system accompanied by all the on stage lights blinking. It looked kind of like paparazzi trying to catch a celebrity on the run except we knew there were no photographers. In rapid succession that flashing crossed the stage, snap, crackle, pop. Just like dominoes falling. For sure it was quick! Every piece of equipment that had previously been glowing with various colors of electric lighting was now dark. And when I say dark, I'm stating that even the tiny lights on every music stand plus our backstage safety light system went out.

Yep.

What felt like minutes, was probably three or four seconds. There was a noticeable electrical buzz through the sound system and except for a couple of building sconces, the back of the stage to the street was dark.

Yes, it was happening folks. In real time!

And while many bands do rent local equipment, this band traveled with their own because well, what else would you expect from the Godfather of Soul? When you're that kind of famous your musicians work only with top-of-the-line custom guitars and amplifiers along the latest in electric keyboards and the hard- to-find 425-pound Hammond B3 organ. Yeah, then there's that.

By sounds and visuals, we knew immediately it was an electrical surge, but as the panicked minutes ticked away, we quickly also discovered that all (as in A-L-L) of the JB Band's personal backline equipment had been fried, hotter than a basket of potatoes in an Air Fryer! So, besides having no musical equipment with which to perform, I had a furious celebrity and inconsolable band members.

Now, up until this time, JB's Manager had been cordial and accommodating but of course, this incident quickly changed everything. He suddenly identified himself as an attorney (!), and his demeanor was exactly as you could expect at that unfortunate moment in time. To my credit as the Director of Operations, I knew the buck stopped with me. We were the production company in charge of this event and had to figure it out. I somehow managed to remain calm, working through the challenge as it was unfolding before us. I also had assistance from our Account Executive who ultimately informed the client there would be "a delay". The conversation with the manager was not easy, and as I recall went something like this:

Our AE: Um, obviously there's been "a situation" here and, um, we're still getting to the bottom of it but, um, meanwhile there will be a *slight delay*. And, um, by "*slight delay*" I mean possibly no show. At all.

JB's Manager: What the **M***er-F***er** is going on here! Or something like that.

Not to mention JB himself was throwing a Godfather-worthy fit. Oh boy! He was quickly escorted back downstairs by his Manager along with directions from me to "give him anything he asks for."

So, JB's Manager kept us waiting quite a few minutes. Maybe he was calming down the star, maybe he was figuring his next move. Fortunately, this allowed me time to problem solve. Could we continue the show? Would JB agree to perform? I met with my team and met with the JB's Musical Director to determine options and a game plan.

When he finally returned, he was insistent that we immediately sign a hastily prepared agreement to replace or repair all the damaged equipment. Further, he commanded that the president of our company authorize and sign his handwritten document.

Did do I need to mention he emphasized *immediately?*

Can't say that I blame him for insisting on that executive signature because even without ever knowing an exact amount, the AE and I already knew we were not authorized to approve this level of an expense which, in our minds, we were guessing could be at minimum double to triple the amount of commission made from a celebrity booking.

Oh, I should add there was one tiny bit of good news in that this was in 1995 and JB did not believe in using electric drums or drum machines or else that would have added substantially to what was already an enormous amount of damages.

So, what happened next? As I mentioned earlier, I already had plenty of musicians on site assisting me with this whole event and, as luck would have it, many of them had personal musical instruments and equipment in their vehicles. Once the "shocks" (pun intended) of what had happened settled in, we had a spontaneous amount of readily available donated equipment that surprisingly JB's Musical Director quickly agreed to use. After all, musicians just want to play music!

My crew wasted no time at all as they quickly removed from the stage the now-fried equipment belonging to JB's band and began reloading the set, running and testing new extension cords along with all the necessary equipment connections and checks.

Oh, and with the open bar flowing and improvised piped-in background music playing (Whew! Small pause as I appreciate that my audio techs always carry a music library.), the guests seemed oblivious to the unplanned on-stage sizzle that had just taken place. Or, at least that's how I choose to remember it.

And eventually our president did show up, signed the mandatory handwritten agreement thrown in his face by JB's manager-now-attorney and, after a liquor-filled two-hour delay, the show went off without another hitch.

As a side note, I'm imagining if this happened in today's fast paced world, the inebriated attendees would have lost patience and gone home or trotted off to an after party (perhaps in the hotel hot tub?) rather than sticking around.

But I will say that the performance was below average because, well, there was that two-hour unlimited liquor thing going on. Even though JB did not drink, his band had been imbibing just as much as the guests, so by now it was all a sloshy blur for everyone.

Except me. This had been a childhood hero, and I was massively disappointed.

So, when we finally sent James Brown and his band back to the hotel, my team was left with the aftermath including assessing the damaged equipment to determine costs to repair or replace along with the responsibility and costs to ship the equipment back to the respective band members.

In the days that followed we were able to dig deeper into the problem and, as they analyzed all the equipment, it turned out the connectors on the industrial extension cables had a faulty design. Further, during that equipment changeover–remember when I mentioned earlier, ahem, that we never advise doing this during live shows?- we learned that a crewmember had stepped on one of those faulty plastic extension cord connections and it broke under his weight. When that happened, the wires inside the connector touched causing the electric surge, thus damaging all equipment on that circuit. Lucky for us, these cords had been rented from a local production supplier with which we had a good working relationship from the many past shows we did together. Since they had supplied all the cables including the extension cords, the responsibility quickly fell to them. So, within a few days, we had our answer. A happy ending for us, but not so much for the manufacturer of those cables who ultimately paid for all repairs and shipping costs due to that newly discovered design flaw.

Lessons Learned:

✓ Select good partners. Above all, this is a relationship business.

✓ Avoid changeovers between sets and really any equipment changes once the stage is set.

✓ No challenge is too great that you cannot find a solution, even under high pressure adverse situations.

✓ Maintain proper insurance coverage for rental equipment

POSITIVE OUTCOMES:

Redundancy matters. I had always included a backup generator as well as additional laptops, thumb drives, cables, etc., but in this case the problem was all in the wiring. From that day forward, I have also added some duplicate items to my ever-growing check list – consoles, controllers, and backline. It was a lifesaver for us that the front of house audio and lighting consoles were on a different electrical feed and not impacted so that night the party could continue. Best of all, my company and my production partner incurred no costs for the damages

CONNIE RILEY BIO: Connie, Vice President for T. Skorman Productions, is a highly honored industry veteran specializing in live stage extravaganzas to fill her clients' bucket lists of requests. From hundreds of performers parading in dazzling sequin costumes to death defying aerialists dangling in mid-air from an oversized balloon to legendary musical celebrities, Connie loves working with entertainers. (Some like the one described above even have sparkle and sizzle!) With a personal background in theatre and performance, Connie has spent years perfecting these dazzling events while cultivating concierge 'backstage-baby-sitting' skills for countless A-List luminaries and wow, does she have some stories to tell! A multiple award winner for her productions, Connie was honored in 2019 receiving the prestigious Klaus Inkamp Lifetime Achievement Award from ILEA, the International Live Event Association, that recognized her decades of volunteer service to the event industry including being a charter member of the ILEA Orlando Chapter as well as serving as the International Association President.

When not on the road, Connie keeps her exciting life in balance by wandering the ten-acre wild jungle oasis she calls home outside of Orlando, FL. She also practices amateur photography while overserving her encounters with Florida's foliage and wildlife, especially turkey, deer, reptiles, and arachnids!

www.tskormanproductions.com

CHAPTER NINETEEN

What Time are July 4th Fireworks in the Land of the Midnight Sun?

By Marianne Schmidhofer, CMM

EDITOR'S NOTE: Marianne is a planning veteran based in Miami, FL, who has a unique background in the cruise industry. This story involves a particular experience she encountered while chartering an entire cruise ship for a client, a common practice in this industry, but something that only a select few highly experienced planners ever undertake due to the extensive negotiations required with cruise ships (not to mention their already established ports-of-call and docking privileges), unique challenges (their public itineraries can be planned years in advance), and variety of variables (hello weather conditions?) when hosting meetings and events at sea as opposed to on land. Oh, and if you're wondering, yes, you usually also need a large sum of money to charter a cruise ship. Just saying.

In her words:

My story has multiple lessons learned. First, do not assume just because it is 4th of July there will actually be fireworks wherever your ship is docked–even in US waters! And second, never underestimate the forcefulness and power of wind, especially while on board a cruising ship! You are probably asking yourself what do these things have to do with meetings and events? Well, this is where my story begins.

As part of my negotiations for a **full ship charter*** in Alaska during the first week of July, the client wanted to assure there would be fireworks on the fourth for all their guests to enjoy. In working with our **ship operations team***, they came up with a wonderful **custom Alaskan itinerary*** to ensure the group would be in the capital city of Juneau on July 4th. According to this itinerary, our ship could stay in port until 10pm to see what was anticipated to be a unique and spectacular Alaskan firework display over the harbor in which our own cruise ship was docked and then still be able to make it to the next scheduled port the following day. The client was thrilled with what we had presented, so the deal was executed.

But this is where the story gets muddy.

The planning of the charter began as per normal operations with details such as gathering the passenger manifests, working on detailed itineraries for days at sea and day excursions while at port, and everything else that needs to get done to accommodate 1400 passengers. We appeared to be sailing along (no pun intended) until we made the necessary request to the port authorities in Juneau to have the ship docked until 10pm on July 4th. It was only then that we learned there would be no fireworks that evening because (as everyone in Alaska, but apparently not everyone at the Miami cruise headquarters, knows) it does not even get dark up there until almost midnight! So, while they do have a firework display, in order to say it's on July 4th, it is done at midnight on July 3rd which technically makes it held on July 4th. Further, due to our custom itinerary, which once applied for must be adhered to down to the last minute, our ship would not even arrive at the port until 8am July 4.

Ooops!

Second, we learned even if we were allowed to change our schedule the port authority could not allow us to dock as the fireworks are staged and shot off from the end of the pier our ship would be at, plus having a ship as large as ours docked there would block the fireworks view for the residents.

Wait, what?

We had to come up with another way to celebrate the 4th of July for this charter without giving a big disappointment to our clients' guests, all of whom were US Citizens and used to enjoying that traditional 4th of July firework extravaganza. After weeks of considering all kinds of options, and I mean everything was on the table for discussion, we discovered a laser light company who would build a large screen on the top deck and create a custom July 4th laser light show. This seemed like a unique and fabulous substitution, so we presented the idea to the client who thought it was awesome. Problem solved. Whew! In truth, we were all pretty excited about the idea as it was different yet seemed patriotic in an updated sort of way as the graphics that were produced and the accompanying music were amazing.

After some juggling that required major muscle movements and all-around finagling to accommodate and store the required special ordered equipment, we managed to get it all on the ship in time for departure. Once the cruise departed Seattle the production team worked two days straight to install the lasers, screen, and rest of the paraphernalia required to produce a show of this nature, all outside on the top deck. This also had to be done in keeping with the Captain's request that the equipment all be tightly secured, not be a visible eyesore to the passengers, nor be an obstacle to any normal ship activities that our passengers might be enjoying. Believe me, safety and security concerns are always first. The challenges and restrictions for accomplishing our task kept mounting, but finally the day came when we were fully inspected, approved, and ready for the big event.

Thus far the cruise had been going smoothly, and as the ship began to depart the port of Juneau at the required time of 10PM, we were ready to have our custom-built laser show on our privately charted cruise right before midnight. As we began to pick up speed in our port departure the terribly expensive and huge wide screen on the top deck became unstable. The production crew rushed to secure it while simultaneously getting additional support from various ship crew members. Then our worst nightmare began to happen. The top of that screen began to rip. As I remember, it was kind of like one of those slow-motion movie scenes except this was in real time. Happening right before our eyes. Seriously! Simultaneous to our attempt to get the screen down in one section it was already shredding into a million pieces. The shock and disbelief on the production team's face said it all. We have seriously damaged equipment and a laser light show to perform in less than 2 hours. Now what are we going to do?

Canceling was not an option. As we stood in silence and disbelief on the top deck taking in the surreal scene in front of us, one of the observant techs noticed that all the railing around the top deck was made of flat white panels. Thinking quickly on his feet, he immediately proposed we try to project the laser graphics onto that surface which ran the entire length of the deck, in essence putting the passengers in the center of the planned laser light show which would be happening all around them. Miraculously, in as quick as it took to say, "let's do it!" we got the approval from ship's management team and instantly started to redirect those projectors from the now missing wide screen to the top deck's railings. Suffice it to say I have never seen a production team work so fast and furious! And of course, there was no time for rehearsals as excited guests had already started to gather in the open-air decks below as well as on our top deck work areas for their much-anticipated patriotic midnight spectacular.

The mood was electrifying as the sun finally set in Alaska that midnight and our Cruise Director welcomed everyone before introducing the show. Trust me when I tell you that the production team and entire cruise staff were all praying to the Spirits high above us in that spectacular Alaskan sky when the music started. To our amazement (and dare I say, relief?) the show went off without a hitch, and by all accounts was fantastic. The guests loved it, most without even knowing about the missing wide screen.

As we, the staff and crew, sighed in relief, disbelief, exhaustion, and pride after the big finale we had seemingly just pulled out of a magician's hat, I couldn't help but think to myself, "well that was *just another day in my life as a meeting and event planner!*"

Or was it? Yes of course!

But one thing I now know for sure is that you always need to expect the unexpected and plan to be challenged beyond your wildest imagination every day of your life in this industry!

*Full Ship Charter: this is when a client does a complete buy out of every cabin and all space on a cruise ship. It involves many unique details such as taking that specific ship out of the normal public passenger rotation for sales as well as mapping out a custom itinerary based on the purchaser's desired ports of call in which the cruise ship may or may not already have established port privileges. (And yes, to be clear, it also involves a whole lot of money.)

*Ship Operations Team: for a private ship charter, the following senior management would, at minimum, typically be included: Director of Charter, Meeting & Events, Vice President of Sales, Director Port Operations, Director Revenue Management, Senior Counsel and sometimes President of Company. The shipboard staff usually remains onboard unless the client requests a particular Captain, Cruise Director or Cruise Staff. In addition, some shore-side staff may travel on the full ship charter to assist with the operations of the special programming.

*Custom Alaskan Itinerary: when a client charters a particular ship, they have plenty of options to customize their daily schedules, always staying in compliance with local dock restrictions regarding arrival and departure times, distance to the next port, etc.

MARIANNE SCHMIDHOFER BIO: With names like Norwegian Cruise Lines, Miami CVB, and Maritz Travel in her employment history, Marianne has literally traveled the world in both a sales capacity as well as that of an experienced meeting planner. She includes working the 2016 Rio de Janeiro Olympics as one of the (many) highlights of her industry work, and oh, the stories she has to tell about that one! She is currently an independent planner and also an adjunct Professor teaching Meeting & Event Management at Florida Atlantic University. In her leisure time she rescues dogs and cats. Presently two dogs and 12 cats, and from her Miami base has successfully lived through more hurricanes than she wants to remember.

https://www.linkedin.com/in/
marianne-schmidhofer-cmm-45a0aa5/

CHAPTER TWENTY

Tower of Terror

By Tracey Smith, CMP, CMM

It was the early 1990s and this was my very first **user confer-ence*** to plan and execute. I had planned other kinds of meet-ings and was super excited to work on this three-day software conference for about 750 tax professionals. Lots of breakout sessions each day, many computers in constant use, various meal and social functions scattered throughout the program so I was exhausted from the hours it took to coordinate all the moving parts.

MINOR DETAIL: We were meeting in New Orleans over the Halloween holiday.

The good news is NOLA is a great babysitter for attendees. All the food and party one could want, all within walking dis-tance of most convention venues including ours.

We used a major hotel on Canal Street for the conference and due to the holiday, we were able to get creative in the planning stages for every aspect of what would be happening before, during and after our daily meeting agenda. Like many planners, we often found ourselves paying particular attention to the details of the conference opening reception with the goal of providing wow factors and making it a memorable kick-off event. The location for ours was a gorgeous, expansive ballroom on the hotel's eighth floor which provided massive floor-to-ceiling windows allowing for a spectacular city view and, being good planners, we thoughtfully added free-flowing beverages to keep everyone warm and happy. All night. Overall, a stunning setting.

Following through on the Halloween theme, we were able to add unique touches such as using dead flowers as centerpieces (that was fun to order from the local florist!) and going full throttle decking out pumpkins in spooky finery. We even hid a live person under a food buffet table with a costumed "pumpkin head" showing as a centerpiece and boy, did he ever have fun scaring the wits out of many attendees as they reached for appetizers.

TRUTHFUL FACT: Yes, planners do things like this and think it is pretty awesome to scare the living daylights out of our attendees!

Now this ballroom happened to be the only room on the eighth floor and the elevators empty into a large foyer. It was big enough that we could decorate the area as a graveyard with live characters such as Elvira, a fantastic witch, and of course, Frankenstein, all of whom greeted guests in character as they arrived. (Pause while remembering the good old days when I had an actual budget that allowed for some fun at these events!) To increase the drama factor to this scene, we even added colored lights and dry ice for that spooky cemetery feel. Yes, it was creating the perfect experience for guests! Just as we had hoped and planned, our photographer captured many fun moments like Elvira cozying up to the company president and Frankenstein carrying one of the VPs into the reception, so everyone was truly able to get into the fun and whimsy of the moment.

At some point, I realized I had left something vitally important in my room, which was on the 29th floor of the hotel, so I left the reception and rode the elevator to the top of the building, and here is where my little story takes another interesting turn. **OLD TIMEY PLANNER DETAIL TO INCLUDE FOR THE NEWBIES READING THIS:** In the early nineties, we did not have cell phones (yes, that is a true fact!), although we did use incredibly attractive and bulky walkie-talkies which made a clear fashion statement as we wore them on our belts (um, no?). To say the least, they worked but had a limited range for coverage. Clearly the earlier version of having a cell phone but no accessibility.

Anyway, once in my room, I grabbed the item I needed and headed back to the elevator bank only to find, well, surprise, surprise! All the hallway lights including the big sign next to the bank of elevators were flashing "fire alarm!" Naturally, this deactivated the elevators and is why I made mention, above, about the limited range capabilities of those walkie-talkies. I was essentially up a crick (or creek, depending from where you hale) without a paddle or, if that is not plain enough, I was on the top floor of an apparently burning hotel with no apparent escape route! In fairness, I did consider the obvious option of running/walking down the stairs, at least for a panicked, New York second. But then I spotted a hotel house phone (yes, these really did exist back then) and thought, "what if…?" while grabbing and listening, praying for a dial tone. And here is what I recall of that brief and panicked conversation:

ME to OPERATOR: "I'm on the 29th floor–is the hotel on fire?" (But what I was really thinking was, *"am I going to die here?"*)

OPERATOR: "Well as best we can tell it appears there is a fire in our ballroom on the eighth floor, but I don't think you need to panic yet. Some smoke got into the elevator shaft and set off all the alarms, but it might be contained there in the ballroom. Or not. We're just not sure yet. But the fire department is definitely on the way!"

ME: Gulp. Nearly fainting, but attempting to stay calm, because, well, that is what planners always do, right? EXCEPT THIS WAS ME AND WHEN SHE MENTIONED "BALLROOM" I REALIZED THAT *FIRE* WAS PROBABLY MY EVENT! Oh, and as a reminder, *I was stuck on the 29th floor with no way to see what was going on.* Well, except for taking the stairs.

ME TO OPERATOR: *"Well dandy!"* (Okay, maybe I used another term. . .) "That's MY group in that ballroom! What do you think I should do?"

OPERATOR: "Um, take the stairs? Or I guess you could wait it out until the fire department gets things under control?"

I proceeded to frantically pace the floor for what seemed like an eternity, trying to reach out via that hotel house phone and my now totally useless trusty walkie but of course, no one responded. They were all in the reception having a *great time* putting out that fire, or so I imagined.

Fortunately for me that eternity quickly came to an end and the elevators began to run again, so I bravely took the first one to the eighth floor. What I found was even more surprising. There was no smoke or fire, but definitely quite a few befuddled and amused people. It turns out that dry ice vapors (remember when I mentioned earlier *that* creative meeting planner's touch we thoughtfully added to our Halloween theme. Oye!) resemble actual fire smoke, so when they wafted into the elevator shaft, the detectors assumed it was a fire. Yep, as in the real deal.

And here is another fun fact we learned that night: when the alarm is triggered, the elevators immediately plunge to the ground floor. With or without passengers onboard. Yikes!

Thankfully, no one was hurt, and we had no viable damage, but rest assured many of our attendees left that evening with some great stories to tell.

Of course, most of those stories were 'not exactly' how we wanted our conference to be remembered!

Oh, and as for me after that night? I'll be okay. Someday.

*__user conference:__ this type of meeting is restricted to actual users of a software application manufactured by a particular company as opposed to a meeting that is open to anyone interested in learning about that product. User conferences are common in the computer/software community and almost always are sponsored by the manufacturer of product so users can better understand the use and applications of the product. The conference also helps retain those users for future versions of the application.

Lessons Learned:

- ✓ Ask more questions than you think you need to ask. None of us, including the decorating company that supplied the dry ice, had an inkling that the ice vapors could drift into the elevators "tricking" the alarms into thinking it was a fire source.
- ✓ Be aware of your surroundings in all situations because you just never know what crazy things may

be in store for you. Turn over every stone; look in every cranny.

✓ Think carefully, very carefully before adding dry ice to your event. Things can happen!

TRACEY SMITH BIO: Tracey is a semi-retired veteran meeting planner who cannot seem to get this industry out of her life. For more than two decades, she planned conferences and other corporate meetings for a division of Thomson Reuters and various corporate meetings for American Express Global Business Travel. Then, she landed her dream job as the Executive Director of SPIN (Senior Planners Industry Network), a network of senior-level meeting planners in North America. Now residing in her 'semi-retired' status in Texas with her husband and precious dogs, Tracey is still active in many industry forums that enable her to stay professionally involved-on her terms-and avoid all that housecleaning.

https://www.linkedin.com/in/
tracey-smith-cmp-cmm-9482361/

Chapter Twenty-One

Fun with Events in the Philippines

By Marjorie Trott, CMP

EDITOR'S NOTE: This is a series of three stories, all of which occurred while the author, Marjorie, was living and working in her home country of the Philippines. At the time, in the early 2000s, her position was that of an Associate Director of Events at the InterContinental Manila Hotel which was one of the only five-star hotels in the country during this time frame, thus it received plenty of international diplomatic business that took place both on site at the hotel and also via contract catering work with surrounding embassies. The hotel has since closed, but oh, what great stories came out of it during the height of its' glory days!

Living Through the Not-So-Rebellious Coup d'état

Coups d'état (attempts to overthrow the government, usually by military force) were unnaturally common in the Philippines for most of the 2000's. The country's first decade of the new millennium saw a total of five military attempts to overthrow the government. Exciting times indeed for any of us living there, and this is my story about one such attempt.

July 26, 2003 started as any Saturday for me would. I had a small trade mission group arriving from the US that afternoon, and after I made sure their check in had gone smoothly, I met up with girlfriends for a usual Saturday night social of drinks after dinner. On this night it was even more drinks, then home. I'm sure you get the picture.

The InterContinental Hotel where I worked, was right at the heart of Manila's Central Business District and was considered a part of Luxury Row, an area known for hotel chains such as ours plus the Shangri-La and Peninsula to name a few. There were also plenty of haute couture fashion houses along with the trendiest bars and restaurants located close by in what was known as the Greenbelt Entertainment District. This is where my friends and I chose to hang out most Saturday nights and tonight was no exception. It was also a stone's throw from my hotel.

Which is exactly why I mention having returned to the hotel after saying goodbye to my friends around midnight in order to use the lady's room before boarding the MRT (our above-ground rapid rail line) as the station was right behind our building. During my brief stop I ran into our Director of Security, Pete, who was also the Overnight Manager on Duty that weekend. He reported that so far it had been a pretty slow night in spite of running a solid 90% occupancy that evening.

Famous last words.

As I left Pete in our lobby to go catch my train home, something happening just outside caught both our eyes and caused me to quickly sober up. Since our lobby doors were all glass, we could clearly see about ten to twelve men dressed in military uniform heading towards our hotel driveway. Pete didn't skip a beat as he handed me the keys to those precious glass doors and then said, "The lock is at the bottom of the door. I'm going out to meet them and you just be sure to lock these doors while I'm out there talking to them."

A little bit scary, but okay. I knew that Pete was a military and police veteran before joining the normally safe world of hospitality, and I trusted that he knew what he was doing.

Just as I knelt to reach the lock of the heavy doors, I could see Pete shake hands with one of the soldiers noting with relief that so far, they were all smiling. That had to be a good sign, right?

Then as I continued watching, a black beret-wearing older-looking soldier that I assumed to be a senior officer emerged from the group and also shook Pete's hand, this one more strongly as his other hand grasped Pete's shoulder for an additional side hug. Then with a little more chatter and a wave at Pete, the soldier appeared to gather his men before they all turned to leave. I waited until Pete was almost at the door before unlocking them to let him back in. "What's up?" I nervously asked.

My answer came as he coolly reached down to re-lock the doors behind him and then took out his radio, changed the dial to "1" - which goes out to all our radio-users – before calmly announcing, "Code Red," our internal code for hotel lockdown. He quickly followed that with "This is not a drill!"

Okay then!

Cool-as-a-cucumber Pete went on to explain to me that those were the soldiers, discovered earlier in the week, to have abandoned their posts. Without saying it out loud, we both knew our government had immediately issued a taskforce to look for them since there were reports that they were plotting a coup d'état. In fact, we learned later on in the week that earlier during the same evening and before showing up in our drive-way they raided the Army Constabulary to steal additional guns and explosives. Yep, they were the real deal all right!

As if reading my mind, Pete went on to explain. "I went to the military academy with one of them. That's what made them turn around and spare our hotel and keep it out of any mutiny plans." Then he quickly started calling his counterparts at the Shangri-La and Peninsula hotels providing a much needed and appreciated warning since he knew it was just a matter of time until those men would end up there.

"Now, please go home," Pete instructed. "As long as the hotel is on lockdown, we will be safe. That group is likely to leave the city and hide out until this all blows over because now everyone – including the government taskforce - knows they are right here."

Exhausted from both my earlier partying with friends and this drama at my hotel, I did as I was told and went home. And the last thing I remember thinking before I fell asleep was how grateful I was that Pete had protected our hotel. It seemed he had successfully talked those guys into going elsewhere and at that point I assumed the armed militia would leave the city completely while I finally got a good night's sleep.

So, it was with great surprise that I heard the rest of the story as soon as I woke up that Sunday morning. As I sleepily reached for coffee while also searching for my phone, I found my mother with an intent gaze fixed on the TV, apparently watching breaking news. Seeing me up at last–it was only 9AM, mom!-she mumbled something about my phone ringing and beeping with messages since 6 o'clock that morning. She was convinced it was because that breaking news was happening right at the building across the street from our hotel.

What?!

I made another quick attempt at sobering up while realizing I had about twenty missed calls and voicemails, with a similar number in text messages, and the news was not good.

Having been peacefully turned away from the InterContinental and the other luxury hotels they had set their sights on, those soldiers finally stormed across the street and then barged into the nearby Oakwood Residences (technically they are serviced apartments, not that those rebels actually cared what they were invading), quickly taking over that building.

Needless to say, my entire Sunday was spent glued right on the television as the drama kept unfolding before us. At one point the TV video camera panned through the area stopping right smack at the bottom of our hotel driveway where you could clearly see a pack of C-4 explosives all strung together. *Yikes!* Thankfully, our hotel had a separate entrance that was used to evacuate all guests choosing to leave, so I immediately started making phone calls to my corporate clients, assuring them that their guests were being evacuated safely.

Believe it or not, the entire drama-now referred to as the "Oakwood Mutiny"-lasted less than 24 hours. By around 8pm on Sunday evening, the rebels peacefully surrendered without a single casualty nor damage to any property. It was duly noted, however, that during their siege the "outlaws" consumed volumes of sodas, bottled waters and enjoyed prime Angus steaks from the Oakwood pantry. Maybe all they needed was a good (expensive!) hot meal?

And as I went back to work the next day, I was truly expecting our hotel to be closed. To my great surprise I walked in to witness our breakfast restaurant filled to the brim as the majority of our guests (including my prized group of VIPs, the US Trade Mission entourage) declined to be evacuated since they wanted to watch all the *excitement* going on right outside their windows. Plus, there were other curious locals that dropped by the hotel to have breakfast and get a feel of the *exhilaration* of the area from the day before.

People are so strange!

Even my luncheon meeting that day–hosted by the American Chamber of Commerce–had over fifty extra attendees show up; and here I was, expecting for the event to be cancelled because, well, we just had about half a dozen major explosives hooked up at our driveway yesterday. But as the saying goes, *all in a day's work!*

We Are Not Rebels!

After months of business courtship, our hotel had finally won the contract to provide the catering services at the US Embassy compound in Manila. The event was the 226th Marine Corps Birthday Ball, hosted by their local detachment and attended by most of the American community. As one of the most popular annual social gatherings among the ex-pat community, they were expecting around 500 guests because, well, the Marines know how to throw a party.

So, if you know anything about catering you know how much equipment is involved in the setup process, and for us that included bringing tables, chairs, kitchen equipment and plenty of other non-perishable items from the hotel to our makeshift kitchen onsite at the Embassy. And all that had to be done early in the day before the final food and beverage drop which is made much closer to the event start time making for an extremely strict timeline for the brigade of trucks needed to go back and forth all day long. And remember, our head count for this prestigious event was over 500 attendees, meaning we had our work cut out for us from the start of the morning until the close of the night.

Further, even though the InterContinental Manila Hotel was less than ten miles away from the Embassy, the traffic jams in that area were legendary. This was because The Embassy was located along the popular Roxas Boulevard that overlooked the iconic Manila Bay making for constant bottlenecks and snail-paced traffic as everyone–tourists and locals–slowed down to enjoy that magnificent vista.

Earlier in the day our deliveries seemed to be going like clockwork and I must say at this point I was feeling kind of proud of how everything was going, that is until it stopped going well. Completely. Let me explain.

I was riding in the truck with our last delivery of non-perishables before the final run back to the hotel for the star attractions-all the food and beverage coming fresh from our hotel kitchen. We were even about a half hour ahead of our anticipated schedule with this truck when we rolled in at the embassy gates and, as we had been doing all morning, my team was required to stop and provide their credentials to get through the thick layers of embassy security. That's when my former feeling of accomplishment quickly vanished. A lean and handsome official looking gentleman sporting a polo shirt bearing the US seal on its' left breast pocket, wearing both dark glasses and an earpiece along with a very intimidating sidearm came out of nowhere and barked, "State your business!"

As this was a new "greeting" (plus we assumed perhaps he was unaware of the big party taking place at his embassy that evening?), I disembarked the stopped truck to meet him head on. I then offered a handshake while confidently introducing myself and, getting no response from the armed guard, proceeded to explain what was going on. I proudly told him that the Inter-Continental Hotel was catering the Marine Ball that evening assuming that would be our golden ticket through the gate.

Instead, he blatantly ignored me while boldly stepping inside our 24-foot truck which was filled to the brim with the remaining equipment. "You'll need to take these out," he barked, as I'm sure I jumped just a little in surprise.

Not sure if I heard him right, I responded with a simple, "Take what out, sir?"

"Everything! This truck needs to be emptied so we can run each item through the detector and inspect the inside of the truck." As he shouted orders, I knew this guy meant business.

Blood was already rushing to my face which I guess is what empowered me to respond in kind, not even realizing I was stepping into his personal space as I responded. "Let me get this straight. You are telling me that we are to unload close to a ton of hotel equipment on this hot pavement (it was already a scorching 100°F that day), then wait while you *attempt* to run each piece through your detector, which I can already tell you none of it will fit. Then we would be expected to load it back into the truck, drive through the gate and park, only to take it out again so we can continue with our set up for this evening's gala? Is THAT what I understand you are asking me, Sir?"

To my surprise, Mr. Hotshot stepped back a little, perhaps not expecting any resistance coming from someone half his size, not to mention a woman. But I could not back down now as the adrenaline was flowing. Plus, to the surprise of every-one–including me-within earshot now gathered around us to witness this confrontation at the Embassy gates, I was already on my tiptoes and all up in his face!

"And, if we do this, sir, you should know that we will most definitely not be able to start the Marine Ball on time tonight." Now my own face was three shades of red. Mostly because it was it was so dang hot at 3 o'clock that afternoon, but also because my otherwise perfectly planned event day was about to come to a halt, all because of some unknowing big shot security guy.

Sensing, if only a tad, that he was messing with the wrong woman (at least that is how I now choose to remember it), Mr. Big-Stuff did take a small step back before he continued. But I could tell by his stoic stance he was not about to back down. He met my glare while offering this. "Ma'am, there was a group of rebels that sieged the Ambassador's residence in South America not long ago."

Oh yea. There was *that*.

He gave me a quick minute before smugly continuing. "And ma'am, did you know they had posed as caterers in order to enter the compound?"

Gulp. Did I just see his eyebrow raise a little as his head cocked?

"Sir," I composed myself and calmly began a rebuttal as I recalled hearing about that terrible incident in the news. "I can appreciate your concern, really I can. But that incident took place in a very remote area where that Ambassador's residence was located. We are in the middle of Manila on Roxas Boulevard, only a block away from the Philippine Police Constabulary. There are over a thousand people here at your doorsteps, milling around in the middle of a hot day. My team has been dropping off equipment since 8 o'clock this morning, without any incident. We work for one of the largest *American* Hospitality companies, putting together a party for the United States Marines. May I assure you, Sir. We. Are. Not. Rebels."

And with that he abruptly turned around, but I swear not before I saw a slight smirk on his face at having listened to my discourse. Then we all watched as he dialed a number on his mobile phone, and I learned later he spoke with my client who happened to be the Marine Detachment Commander. To those of us who could hear, there were some definite words thrown during that lengthy exchange during which time I made a point of looking at my watch several times. Two can play this game!

Finally, Mr. Scowl-Face turned around and said "OK, you may go in, but I'm going to have to be in the venue while your team sets up".

Offering what probably appeared to be an insincere smile and drawing upon my utmost patience (even though deep inside I was terrified this long delay would cause us to push back the all-important gala start time) I replied, "That would be perfectly fine, sir. Thank you."

And at the end of the night the Marine Ball lived up to its reputation of being the most fun gala event that season. Held both inside and outside in the Chancery's elegant garden, it seemed no matter where I walked on my rounds that evening, I would catch a glimpse of my new "friend", almost always still scowling and usually wiping sweat off his forehead while guarding that oh-so-hot and crowded gala.

But at one point, I witnessed one of our servers offer the man a cold bottle of water and I swear he smiled at that simple gesture. And I can assure you that after experiencing the run around as we successfully catered our very first event that night at the US Embassy, I made a point before any future ones to always send a courtesy email to Mr. Strict-Pants ahead of our arrival and thank him in advance for not requiring us to empty out our truck with every delivery.

Hopefully, that made him smile again, too.

You Want Me to Do What? A Fun Story About When Your Job Description Gets Stretched!

The British Ambassador to the Philippines was a well-known patron of the theatre arts, and often invited the local

Manila repertory to perform during receptions at his residence. In my position with the hotel, I was the main contact when the Ambassador needed outside catering services delivered to his residence, and this particular event was going to be in honor of a rather famous British Theatre Guild that was currently touring throughout Asia. I was told by his staff that the Ambassador was especially excited to host this prestigious group from his homeland, and we all knew their popularity was growing with each stop of the Asian tour.

So, on the initial phone call to my office, I learned that the Embassy would be holding a special reception in their honor and that The Guild would be performing in front of a VIP audience full of members from the diplomatic community along with various hand-selected special guests. Further, it was determined that the performance would take place in the residence's large living room and the audience would be seated on chairs arranged in an oval, two rows deep with the actors performing in the middle making it a very intimate gathering. But with this type of space requirement, when the invitation list grew to over 100 guests it was agreed that the event would have to be spread over two nights.

Since all twelve Guild members (eleven actors and one narrator) were staying at our hotel I got to know them and had the pleasure of watching their multiple rehearsals at the ambassador's residence, always with an eye toward making sure the overall event flow was paced with our selected food and beverage service. To my surprise, they even included me in decisions regarding staging cues, entrance and exit flows, audience blocking (as they had no backstage), and other production details. I must admit it was wonderful to be included in all the major and minor details surrounding this event, but that was quite normal to my job. What was unusual was the bond I felt with this group, and it was truly a joy to get to know them and be able to watch their performances.

The first night went off without a hitch. Guests started arriving at 6:30pm and enjoyed a one-hour cocktail reception before taking their seats to marvel at the spectacular fifty-minute performance, the highlight of their evening. During the show I noticed that the narrator's speech sounded weak, as if she were losing her voice. So naturally, at the end of the play that night, I gave her a cup of ginger tea at which time she commented that she was indeed nursing a bit of a cold, most likely due to all that travelling. Apparently, their busy performance schedule was all finally starting to affect both her energy level and performance ability but as with most performers they always tried to press through those personal challenges for the sake of their shows.

The next morning, I came fully prepared to further assist her and brought a supply of throat lozenges plus more ginger tea, and during rehearsal she already sounded better.

But that evening, while the pre-performance cocktail reception was going on, a panic-stricken Social Secretary of the Ambassador rushed up to me reporting that the narrator had completely lost her voice.

"Oh my! What's going to happen? What can I do to help you right now?" At that moment I could only think of questions with no apparent answers.

But to my complete surprise, the Ambassador's clever Social Secretary already had it all figured out. Or so she thought. "You! Dear, you have a lovely narrator voice, and you pretty much know the play since you've been with us every step of the way during rehearsals and such."

"Me? Why me?"

Then, as if on cue her panicked and now pleading voice started to crack just a little (perhaps for dramatic effect on my behalf?) before she went on to say, "I'm sure you can step in and fill her shoes, can't you? Please?"

"Um, sure thing?" I responded with no confidence at all since my mouth was speaking without direction from my brain. Never a good combination.

No matter how uncomfortable I personally felt at that moment, there was only ten minutes to show time, so the pressure was on. Like a tiny deer when confronted by those shocking headlights, all eyes were now focused on me. I nervously took the script, threw back a shot of something strong (for fortification, of course), told myself not to faint, and discovered the true meaning of "the show must go on!"

And of course, as I took that final deep breath and steadied my performance legs while stepping into the spotlight, the first person I noticed sitting in the front row of that oh-so-intimate setting was my boss, the hotel general manager. Earlier, before I was recruited as the "ingenue narrator," I witnessed him scanning the crowd looking for me, presumably to tell me for the umpteenth time that I missed a crinkle on the cocktail linen. So, it was actually a little bit fun for me to watch his eyes widened as I found my professional voice and started to narrate the play.

And then just when I thought I was getting my "look at me, I'm an actress!" tempo on a roll, my part was over, and the real performers resumed doing what they do best to carry the rest of the show. But in that fleeting moment as I left the spotlight, I did see my boss's face break out in a wide grin and, just like a giddy stage father, he gave me the two thumbs up of his approval.

It goes without saying that in the end, I was certainly not ready to give up my day job as Associate Director of Events-just yet! But I was pretty darn proud of my amateur accomplishment, and more than a little relieved that I did not mess up an otherwise well-rehearsed professional production.

It was another lesson for me that as event pros in this industry, we truly do wear many hats and never know which one we will be asked to wear, or in this case, what script we'll be holding in our hands to make sure the client's "show will go on!"

MARJORIE TROTT BIO: With a hospitality career that started in her homeland of the Philippines, Marjorie is now Associate Director, Meetings & Special Events at a luxury resort complex in Orlando, FL. Her path from Manila to Orlando also included stops at The Peabody Memphis and one of the largest convention center Hyatt Hotels in their worldwide network. With a trained eye on details and diplomatic protocol, Marjorie has worked some amazing events, large and small, but it was those years working with the Embassies in Manila that has provided many of the most interesting stories during her career path.

https://www.linkedin.com/in/marjorie-trott/

CHAPTER TWENTY-TWO

A "Swinging" Start to This Convention

By Dick Wilson

In the 1980s big production numbers at conventions were all the rage. Often elaborate and expensive, they could involve singers, dancers, and other performers in choreographed musical productions. And this custom-designed opening had it all. Superb lighting. Punchy music. Beautiful scenery and seasoned professional performers. Oh yeah, and special effects too.

I'm sure they had a great dress rehearsal. But that actual performance on opening day? Well, that was another story.

The setting of this extravaganza took place in a large modern theater built for live performances. This particular audience consisted of hundreds of auto franchise owners gathered for their annual convention. Lively music blasted away while attendees took their seats. Excitement was intense, just exactly what the planners had hoped for.

The lights dimmed, the crowd hushed, and the opening number began. The curtain slowly parted, revealing the stage set—a huge vertical "Hollywood Squares" style grid, with costumed dancers posed and silhouetted in each square. They began moving in unison to the recent pop hit, "Magic" by Olivia Newton-John.

The male performer in the center square put a microphone to his lips and began to sing. All went well for the first few bars of the song. Until…

The singer got to the line "You have to believe we are magic; nothing can stand in our way."

Except something did stand in his way. This was the point where he was supposed to step off the grid and literally fly around the stage. He was rigged to do that. But that clearly did not happen.

On the plus side, he also did not fall to his death at this point. That said, if you are picturing a guy literally suspended in air, helplessly swinging in the breeze, with thousands of eyes focused on him, your imaginary vision is correct. Peter Pan he was not. More like a singing pendulum.

To his credit, he was an unflappable performer. Somehow, he was able to continue singing while uncontrollably swinging back and forth, still attached to the flying apparatus. This is what might commonly be referred to as a technical glitch. What a glitch it was!

The music played on. To the credit of the other dancers still in their grid squares, they too kept doing what they were supposed to do. But I'm sure everyone onstage was hoping and praying for any kind of intervention, divine or otherwise.

Mercifully, the curtain came down, probably less than a minute into the dangling/singing/swinging male vocalist's not-so-finest flight after which the audience heard "Ladies and gentlemen, please welcome your president…" And just like that the show went on.

And regardless of what the president said that morning, there was probably only one topic of conversation at lunch that day.

> **Lessons Learned:**
>
> ✓ Even with successful rehearsals, in live productions anything goes!

DICK WILSON BIO: Dick recently retired from a 20-year career as a freelance event producer and scriptwriter. Before that he was Director of Sales Conferences for Tupperware US where he wrote, produced, and executed multiple regional and national conferences annually for a nationwide sales force of over 80,000. Today he is frequently seen happily strumming one of his many ukuleles, while reflecting back on his crazy past life in which he actually enjoyed being the boss. When everything went right, that is.

https://www.linkedin.com/in/dick-wilson-59436615/

Chapter Twenty-Three

Bonus Short Stories

Author's Note: Thanks for reading this far! As I collected stories for this book, I realized that some were longer and chock full of necessary details that gave a complete and many times complex snapshot of the unexpected day-to-day challenges for those of us who work in this industry. But some submissions were short, sweet, and still needed to be heard. That's when the idea for this final chapter came about.

And, as you have already learned from reading the previous stories, when it comes to the success or failure of meetings and events, it's all about the management of details. The next stories are quick and fun reads, and all fall under the heading of...

THIS REALLY HAPPENED!

Read on for more true tales from experienced planners who have learned the hard way that you always, always sweat the small stuff!

1

Lady, Where's My Balcony?

By Sherry Colodny

I was working a medical meeting on a Royal Caribbean cruise ship and, having just arrived in my cabin, was unpacking before going down to set up the program's registration. As I was walking out the door, my cabin phone rang delivering a disturbing conversation. The young woman working in the dockside ship check-in area had one of my speakers, a physician, with her and apparently, he was furious, refusing to board the ship until I stop whatever I was doing and come back to the dock to meet him in order to solve his problem.

"You have to fix this. RIGHT AWAY!"

"Okay, let's calm down, doctor. What is the problem here?"

"My cabin doesn't have a balcony, and I refuse to come on board until this is settled. In fact, I refuse to speak at this program unless I have a balcony!"

Lucky for me I was still in my cabin and had easy access to all my paperwork. I quickly looked up the contract this doctor had signed as part of his speaking agreement and was relieved to find out nothing like that had been promised. In fact, there was no mention at all of a balcony being included or even waitlisted in his name. At least I knew the cruise line and I were working within our boundaries by pushing back with this hostile speaker. I proceed to politely inform him of this and urged him to continue on board to fulfill his speaking engagement. He continued to argue about it but eventually gave up at which time I reminded him, politely of course (!), about what time and place he should be meeting up with our group.

About forty-five minutes later he did show up at my registration desk and although he was still a bit argumentative, he had at least calmed down and accepted his fate on this cruise without a balcony. But that is not the end of this story.

Instead of continuing to vocalize his protest, he chose to continue a more silent demonstration by wearing only his swim trunks, flip flops and a very casual island style shirt during the entire cruise, including while giving his formal presentation to the other doctors for which he was paid a handsome sum of money. The nerve of him!

Unfortunately, I felt I was the embarrassed one every time I saw him dressed so casually, but this caused me to check that contract once again. Sure enough, there was no mention of any kind of dress code–who would ever imagine you would need it for a professionally paid speaker?–so lesson learned on that omission!

As with many things in this crazy industry, we really do learn things the hard way, but believe me once is all it took for me before I started incorporating more specifics into those future contracts!

2

Meeting Planner Vs. Mother of the Bride
(Never underestimate adults behaving badly!)

Also by Sherry Colodny

It was a Saturday morning on the last day of a three-day conference. I went down to open the registration desk located in the foyer area outside of the ballroom. To my surprise, although we'd had our registration area set up in that very same location on the previous two days, it wasn't there!

Scratching my head while standing there at that early morning hour (and still without coffee), I glanced around the hotel foyer and noticed what was clearly all of my registration set, at least in the days prior, moved well over to another area nowhere close to my ballroom and meeting set. On further in-spection I even found all my signage and registration materials so that was a relief but still, what was going on here?

I immediately called my convention service manager and ask her to meet me right away in the foyer. Of course, she was horrified and had no idea why everything was moved, but together we quickly picked it all up and reset everything back in its' proper location just as my participants were arriving for their morning session.

We soon learned that there was a wedding taking place in this same ballroom later that day, hours after my program would end at noon. Apparently, the mother of the bride had come down to visit "her" space the previous night and was not happy in seeing "someone else" had laid claim to the exact spot where the pre-wedding photo shoot would be taking place. The nerve! Thus, as she finally confessed to her own hotel service manager, she took it upon herself to move everything out of her way as nothing could be more important to the hotel than her daughter's wedding.

Yeah, right!

And in case you are wondering, yes, that mother of the bride positioned herself in a corner of the foyer looking very unhappy while watching my group *invade her space* as we fin-ished up our conference that morning.

And as for me? When our program ended, I promptly packed up and took the high road as I smiled while passing by her on my exit from the hotel. I am a professional, but no fool and certainly didn't want to stick around to witness any other mother of the bride fireworks since she was watching the clock on our departure!

SHERRY COLODNY BIO: After years executing flawless meetings and events for countless clients, Sherry is now Chief Empowerment Officer for her own life coaching business where she is combining her management skills with marketing, media and operational services into one powerful package that also include professional speaking. You can find her at:

https://www.linkedin.com/in/ssmeetings/

3

Free Ride?

By Cindy Hartner, CSEP

Sometimes you've just got to scratch your head and laugh, and this was one of those times.

We were providing round trip shuttle transportation from a hotel to an off-site venue for a corporate client, so the vehicles were running constantly throughout the event. Apparently at one point, without the driver or field staff's notice, a homeless man boarded one of the busses, meandered all the way to the rear of the bus, found a very comfy position, and then proceeded to ride back and forth all night, sound asleep in the back seat.

Unbelievably (yet thankfully), none of the clients noticed him all evening! This was most likely because with continuous shuttles running all night, they normally don't fill completely on the return so that guests don't have to sit on the motor coaches too long before departure. Also, I'm sure the fact that it was dark and he was blessedly passed out helped his cause which, apparently, was to get a good night's sleep in a warm and safe environment.

So, you can imagine the driver's surprise when, after depositing the last guests at the hotel from his final run, he flipped on the bus lights and started his final walk-through inspection. Normally this only yields items for the client's lost and found box. Except this time when he approached the rear, that homeless man sat up and said, "Hey buddy, where am I?"

That was one shocked driver!

4

Wedding Cake Disaster

Also by Cindy Hartner

Everyone knows that Summer in Texas can be hot. I was working at a country club venue that was extremely popular for wedding receptions due to some gorgeous floor-to-ceiling windows overlooking a rolling golf course. On one occasion, the bride chose not to use a professional baker but instead enlisted a family friend to make her wedding cake, a practice not highly recommend by those of us in the industry, but brides are never wrong, right?

If only!

Now ideally, cakes are not delivered until about one to two hours prior to the event in order to keep them fresh. But as it happened in this case, the family friend-turned-cake pro, ahem, was also attending the actual wedding ceremony meaning she wanted to dump (oops-I meant deliver-did I say dump?) that cake much earlier than normal allowing her maximum time to enjoy the afternoon along with the other invited guests. And that, dear reader, is where this cake story starts a slippery slide...

You see, she made another rooky mistake by using colorful gel icing which is not as stiff as other types of decorative icing (and also why it is not used by professionals, sigh). So, you can probably guess what happened next. Yes, the cake started melting and in no time at all that colorful gel icing looked like a rainbow waterfall draining down the sides of the cake.

Oh, yes it did!

To his credit, my chef rushed out and tried to start triage, but it was already beyond repair. Then, just as we were all nervously huddling around that thing trying to think of some way to salvage it, things got even worse when, right before our eyes, the multiple layers of cake tiers started sliding, too. Yes, really!

Now, to help you visualize this scene, think back to when you were in school and had to do that science experiment making a fake volcano explode in your lab and then you and your friends were all laughing as you watched that colorful goo rush slowly down the sides of your now-ruined display. Yeah, that's how bad this was! That messy *blob* now looked more like a very sad PRIDE volcano than a beautiful wedding cake.

So, when the bride finally arrived, we had to quickly take her aside and explain what happened being oh-so-careful as we showed her the end result. Fortunately, she agreed to the best and most logical solution which was to cut the cake without fanfare much earlier in the itinerary. Not quite as in, "how do you feel about dessert as your first course tonight?", but something similar.

Oh, and that friend who baked the cake? I have no proof of this, but I am pretty sure she never volunteered to bake another cake for a friend again. At least not for a wedding!

NOTE: Cindy's bio and contact information can be found at the end of Chapter Eleven, <u>The Night Hell Froze Over in Texas</u>, her story about working a VIP event during a major Texas ice storm.

5

Don't Leave Passengers Behind!

By Tamiko Kinkade

As you can imagine from the title, this story involves a very embarrassing mistake I made once while managing a client's week-long bus tour on the west coast, specifically visiting lumber-related industries and forests. At the opening reception in Seattle, I explained ground rules that with a group our size, we would all need to be very prompt. I also threatened that, "if you were not on the bus as scheduled, we would leave without you." Of course, that was meant as a general warning to keep the group punctual and not necessarily that we were so strict as to actually do that. Heavens no!

But sure enough, the very next morning-our first of that weeklong tour-it happened. Yep, we left poor Herb and Myrtle behind. In my defense, I counted heads and thought I had an adequate number for departure, but it seems two staff members were counted twice. Plus, I did not even know this until we were crossing the border into Canada to visit British Columbia.

While on the ferry, several other attendees found me and were quite excited as they exclaimed, "They made it!"

"Uh, that's great. But who and what are you talking about?"

I soon heard "the rest of the story" as I discovered that Herb and Myrtle were left back at the hotel due to oversleeping coupled with my unfortunate mistake of counting someone else twice thus thinking my total head count was correct and causing us to pull away without them. But after waking up in a panic, the sleepy couple hailed a cab and caught up with our group just before we boarded the ferry. Overall, they were quite gracious but a little disheveled for the day.

On the plus side, to my knowledge, I have never left anyone behind since!

Communication and Publication Solutions, Inc.
tk@tkcpsolutions.com
http://www.tkcpsolutions.com/

6

Excuse me, Is There a Waiter in the House?

By Terry Matthews-Lombardo, CMP

Ever been in the thick of things with about 1000 hungry attendees ready to walk through the doors and enjoy their luncheon only to learn–*surprise!* -that the convention center's union wait staff had just walked off the job? Yes, this really happened, and fortunately for us the tables were ready, salads pre-set, entrees were stacked on the rolling racks, and the convention center's management team rallied big time along with every able-bodied member of my own staff to serve our guests just as fast as we could spring into action. In fact, even more amazing, was that the whole lunch service only took an extra 40 minutes beyond the originally allotted time which was not bad work for amateur servers! Further, during the scramble we managed to alert the after-lunch general session speaker and moved his talk right into our chaotic banquet venue allowing us a breather to leave those dirty dishes on the tables while the conference continued on "as if we'd *planned* it that way."

Yeah right, wink-wink!

Post Thoughts: If you are a planner or food service professional, I know you are thinking that leaving dirty dishes on the table during a speech is a big no-no. Also, an even bigger *ewww*, right? But keep in mind that this was a panic-driven situation and not a normal one. We did what we had to do including renegotiating with the speaker to move him into that chaotic ballroom scene, and at that moment in time it worked.

Also, having no advance notice of the walk-out (we found out later it was an unauthorized, unorganized attempt at a union rally), we simply did what we had to do to put the food in place, and that included a cry for *"All hands on deck,* NOW!" from our management as well as from the venue's remaining management team. We did feel fortunate that at least the food was prepped and ready to serve before that walk-out happened.

And if you're wondering what happened to the thousands of dirty dishes at the end of our program? Rest assured we left each and every one in place for the center to deal with once we vacated that ballroom. That's right. *Tag-you're it!*

7

Here Comes A Snake!

Also by tml

So, picture this scene: my group of about 1,000 attendees was in Arizona, having a typical "Wild, Wild West" themed party on a mountainside plateau area made available specifically for group events. This included old-west style props of all shapes and sizes (think cactus, wagons, saloon props and more), an array of cowboys and cowgirls serving the chowdown buffet as well as providing plenty of simultaneous gun totin' rope tricks and other entertainment on multiple stages and venues throughout the event. Sound like fun? Yee-haw yes! That is until it's not.

Our guests were first bussed from their downtown Phoenix hotel locations to the base of the mountain where, as part of the ambience to get them excited about the old West theme night, they had a choice of staying on the bus or jumping onto a hay wagon to make the ascent up the side of the mountain, and this was going very smoothly until the party started winding down and people were doing the reverse in order to leave the mountainside. In fact, almost everyone had already made it down to the base of that mountain to those awaiting busses until one of the very last wagons encountered "a situation."

And by situation, *I mean a snake.*

And if you know anything about horses and snakes, well let's just say they don't really play together very nicely so yes, *all snake-meets-horse-heck broke loose.*

As the event's planner, I was still at the event area closing things down as I heard the emergency call come over our radios. As I recall, it was something like this: "Mayday. *Mayday!* *Arattlerjustspookedahorseandthewagonisnowfreeflowingdown-thesideofmountain!* Passengers are falling out; emergency services on the way."

But what I heard was **"SNAKE!"** which was all I needed to hear before jumping on top of the nearest table before quickly realizing that I was the only one in sheer panic at *my* location.

The rest of the chaos was happening at the base of the mountain. With my attendees, ugh, as that wagon was dropping people left and right, many of whom were landing on dessert cactus and who knows what else. Oh. My. **And did I mention the part about that particular wagon holding many of my executives and their families because yeah, it's always great to make sure your VIPs leave with a bang?** *Well then, there was that, too.*

Post Event Thoughts: I don't even know where to begin. It was a messy ending to a super successful night, for sure, but just like anything else that occurs during the course of an exciting event, you deal with things as they happen. Up until that *snake* showed up, my biggest problem had been earlier in the evening when we ran out of corn bread which I heard about from plenty of angry people!

Over the course of the next several days I made multiple hospital visits to our injured guests, but in the end, *almost* everyone had a crackin' good time not to mention a super great story to tell that went something like this, "Remember that time when we were having a fabulous event in Arizona and that snake spooked the horse ..."

Yep. That was my group!

8

When Your Ice Sculpture Becomes a Lethal Weapon

And yet one more by tml

The event I was working was being held during the month of June in Phoenix, AZ. For some reason, the client was insisting on keeping the opening reception outdoors. Did I mention it was June? In Phoenix? And this might also be a good time to add that, among the other Southwestern desert décor scattered about, the company logo was being prominently displayed via an incredible ice sculpture that was beautifully backlit with the logo colors shining majestically through each of the giant letters. It truly was a gorgeous piece of decoration, that is until about 45 minutes into the two-hour reception.

That's when this two-hundred-pound block of ice felt the full force of global warming, or in our case, the 100-degree Phoenix temp effect. That beautiful company logo made a very graceful exit as it slid, ever so gently, right off the table on which it had been placed. And just like that a $4000 chunk of ice turned into ice cold puddled water.

But wait. That was not even the best part! Want to guess where at least one of those ice letters landed when it crashed? If you answered right on top of someone's foot you would be correct! That poor guy actually suffered a broken foot as a result of this accident but considering the amount of people in close proximity to the sculpture when it made that spectacular crash landing, I'm thinking we actually lucked out with only sustaining one injury.

Lessons learned? You bet! And here they are:

1] We planners like to keep our clients happy, so when this client insisted the reception remain outside despite my objections (none of which included a prediction that "the ice sculpture might melt and break someone's foot," but that's beside the point here), I should have been more persistent to move it inside. In hindsight, which is always enlightening, I should have proposed a split option where some items (perhaps, um, the ice sculpture?) could remain inside and move some of the other miscellaneous props–like, perhaps those that don't react to global warming (!)-to the designated outside area.

2] It takes a village. It really does. And you need to listen to many opinions when it comes to big decisions. There were lots of moving parts to this reception, and while I took full responsibility for it all, I really wished the purveyor of that ice sculpture had taken ownership and voiced an opinion, preferably loudly, during the "keep it in or move it out" discussion.

Terry's brief bio can be found on the back cover, but if you'd like to learn more about her please check out her website at www.terrysworldtravels.com . If you enjoy her writing style, please feel free to subscribe to those infrequent blog posts that are usually entertaining stories about meetings, events, travel adventures, and detours.

You can also connect with TML on LinkedIn

9

All Rise and Eyes on Me, Please!

As told to tml By Bruce Meadows

I was the transportation director for a large convention group, so really working mostly outside on the curbs and bus areas where all that action takes place. But it just so happened that during a brief break I had wandered inside the hotel to cool off a bit and take a quick peak at the opening general session that was about to begin in the massive auditorium full of attendees. As a member of the staff supporting this convention, I had backstage access which is where I had gone to grab a bottle of water and happened to still be standing there right when the "Voice of God" was saying, "Ladies and gentlemen, please rise and salute our American Flag as we recite the Pledge of Allegiance!"

At that exact moment, I noticed that right next to me, propped up against the very back wall in this dark corridor behind the stage where I was trying to take a little break from a very hectic morning was a rather forgotten American flag affixed to a long pole. I guess it was my military reflex that instantly caused me to take a swift glance out onto the stage where all the speakers and VIPs were now rising, and I could already see that a few of them were searching for their missing flag. To say the least, a patriotic boo-boo not to mention an embarrassing miss of protocol on the part of the planning team. In a surprising split-second decision on my part, I grabbed that lonely flag beside me and proceeded to rush it out on stage only to find that I was turned around in the darkness and not able to locate an entrance. I had no other choice but to walk back down that corridor a bit to find an accessible door, and no sooner had I opened it than I realized it was a main auditorium entrance. Further, as it took a few seconds for me to finagle that long flagpole in through the doorway while being careful to not be disruptive (so I thought), I got the surprise of my life when the roving spotlight that had been searching for the missing flag found its' *focus on little ole' me* crashing through that door like one of the three Stooges.

Yep. As a hush began in the audience after all eyes had turned on me in the center of that now focused spotlight, I had no choice but to summon all the dignity I could muster and march forward like a proud boy scout in a parade. With my arms shaking from the weight of this heavy apparatus, I held that flag up high and focused on finding a clear path up to the stage while scared as sh#! that I would end up poking someone's eye out with the pointed end of that golden flagpole.

The happy end to this story is that I did finally make it, in a somewhat dignified manner (even though I was sweating bullets all the way up that aisle), and then eventually up the steps leading to the stage where I had no choice but to remain holding the now-weighing-in-at-a-ton flag upright as the spotlight focused in on my sweat-drenched body, dirty tennis shoes and all.

So, I now have two memories from that particular convention program. One was a sense of extreme pride for having jumped in-way out of my comfort level or assigned duty–to proudly present the American flag during a critical moment at the very start of that major convention.

But that other memory? Let's just say the fact that I was out of breath, sweating profusely, and as I was shocked to discover later while looking at some of the official photos from that week that has helped the day live on forever, unfortunately still wearing a baseball cap during the entire patriotic ordeal. So much for my respectful attempt at heroism!

But at least it wasn't on backwards?!

10

Powerful Palm Pilots!

Another story from Bruce as told to tml~

This program was quite a few years ago at the very beginning of the popularity of Palm Pilots which is also to say long before we had reliable internet. For the uninformed, Palm Pilots were kind of a precursor to cell phones as we now know them, but in the beginning owning one of these was the new "it way" to track your data. Needless to say, if you owned one of these babies you were among the cool kids', especially in the world of business professionals.

This program I was working was over one thousand people in Miami, and the client was known for giving all attendees an expensive and super-technical gift at the start of each conference. This year it was the highly coveted new Palm Pilot, and we were handing them out individually as guests entered the ballroom, so you can imagine how excited they all were when they each discovered what that new toy was.

But-and this is important to the story-as we turned over possession, each attendee was instructed not to open or turn it on just yet.

Once all that swag was distributed and everyone was seated in the ballroom, the keynote speaker kicked things off by explaining the gift and laying the ground rules, which included everyone turning their devices on at the count of three.

"One! Two! Three!" he shouted from the stage. "Go ahead and power up your device!"

And just like that the entire ballroom went dark, which during that dramatic moment everyone mistakenly thought had been staged to coincide with this exciting activity of them powering up. Except that it wasn't!

And not only did that ballroom go dark, the entire hotel lost power, so power up actually meant power off. Everywhere.

Including, as we later learned, all up and down South Beach where our hotel was located. So of course, no presentation took place that day, which was a good thing since the entire keynote program was focused on everyone being able to use their new devices and interact during the show.

I don't recall how long it took before the hotel, and city, power was fully restored, but for sure that was one memorable conference for more than just the attendee swag, which in the end, was referred to as "the gift that kept on giving!"

BRUCE MEADOWS BIO: Bruce is an independent contractor and professional logistics manager with vast experience directing multiple areas of events on-site with attention to detail, budget and timelines. He has an expertise in corporate and sales events along with incentive programs but has also worked numerous executive leadership/board meetings and product launches. For a time, he was even a White House Logistics front man, and wow, we'd sure like some stories from assignment!

https://www.linkedin.com/in/bruce-meadows-4b073352/

11

Don't Let That Women Behind Our Registration Desk Again!

By Dana L. Saal CMP, CAE

As the long-time lead planner for an annual conference, I was the familiar face and primary contact for most conference participants. I'm also hyper-focused on efficiency and an exceptional talker. After attempting to "improve" the registration process when lines were long but instead clogging things up as I was cheerily over-talking to too many people, the registrar "invited" me to never step behind their reg desk again.

Happy ending — I never have, and go figure, it's so much easier for everyone!

12

Quick, I Need 50 More Place Settings!

In an attempt to increase efficiency, our onsite team decided that the registrar could pack up while the rest of us went to the closing banquet. My task was to simply count tickets at the door. How hard could that be? I soon found out that collecting them was easy; counting them was not. Somehow, I counted fifty, yes 50, more than the guarantee which, any planner knows, immediately causes panic. Up went more table rounds! Get some more salads prepped! Find fifty more filets, STAT! (PLANNER SIDENOTE: This does NOT make you a popular person with the kitchen staff!)

My client was anxious, especially when it appeared that there really was no need for all that alarm as our original head count was going to stay the same. So, where were those extra 50 people? Well let's just say that I was never allowed to be the only ticket collector again, or at the least, I would be the one sent to pack up registration instead of being put in charge of head counts. Or ticket-taking. Or tallying numbers of any kind.

Happy ending — despite my unnecessarily wreaking havoc with the kitchen, we were only charged for a handful of those extra sets. Apparently, someone felt sorry for me!

13

That Time I Left My Entire Group Stranded on a Street Corner

In 2010 I planned the annual reunion of the General MacArthur Honor Guard — an elite unit comprised of men selected for their military bearing, intelligence, and physical stature. These guys were well into their 80s. Fortunately they attended with their families who could keep them company while they waited quite a while on a street corner in downtown St. Louis for a coach bus that was never going to arrive because, *ooops*, I scheduled it for the wrong day.

Happy ending — once they were notified of my error, the coach company reached out to another driver that had just finished a different client program, and he was able to save our day. Whew!

Saal Meeting Consulting

dana@saalmeetings.com

https://www.saalmeetings.com/

Professional Designations
as noted in this book:

CAE=Certified Association Executive, accredited by the American Society of Association Executives www.asaecenter.org

CEM=Certified Exhibition Manager, accredited by the International Association of Exhibitions and Events www.iaee.com

CHE=Certified Hospitality Educator, accredited by the American Hotel & Lodging Educational Institute www.ahla.com

CHSP=Certified Hospitality Sales Professional, accredited by the American Hotel & Lodging Educational Institute www.ahla.com

CME=Certified Manager of Exhibitions, [formerly] accredited by the Trade Show Exhibitors Association

CMM=Certified Meeting Manager, accredited by Meeting Professionals International www.mpi.org

CMP=Certified Meeting Professional, accredited by the Events Industry Council www.eventsindustrycouncil.org

CPC=Certified Protocol Consultant, accredited by the [former] International Association of Protocol Consultants

CPCE=Certified Professional of Catering and Events, accredited by the National Association of Catering & Events www.nace.org

CPECP=Certified Protocol Etiquette Civility Professional, accredited by the Global PEC Academy www.globalpecacademy.com

CSEP= Certified Special Events Professional, accredited The International Live Events Association www.ileahub.com

HMCC=Healthcare Meetings Compliance Certificate, accredited by Meeting Professionals International www.mpi.org

PBC=Professional Bridal Consultant [aka Certified Wedding Planner], as accredited by the Association of Bridal Consultants www.abcweddingplanners.com

Attention Meeting and Event Planners and Other Hospitality Industry Professionals!

If this book:

- put a smile on your face, and possibly made you laugh out loud
- sparked some deep thinking about what else goes on during meetings and events
- piqued your curiosity about a career path in hospitality
- caused you to remember some crazy instance from a program you were involved with

Then please consider sharing your "fun" story with others! I'll be covering a series of like-minded adventures in future social media and blog posts and heck, if I get enough, maybe there will even be a "*Meetings Mayhem! Volume Two*" in the future that includes *your* story. As you can tell from the spread of these experiences, nothing is off limits when it comes to client requests, celebrity bookings, attendee demands, and the mistakes that planners will suffer through in real time to make it all happen.

This is your open invitation to share a true and personal "special event" journey of your own. Please contact me (see below for options) so we can chat about your version of *mayhem!* **For sure I'll be listening!**

Email: tml@cfl.rr.com
LinkedIn: https://www.linkedin.com/in/terrymatthewslombardo/
Facebook: https://www.facebook.com/TmlWrites
tweet@tmlwrites and Instagram @tmlwrites

And finally, if you can't get enough of my writing style and sense of humor, please consider following me on my website to read about other amusing travel stories and detours. I pinky-promise not to clog your inbox.
www.terrysworldtravels.com

CPSIA information can be obtained
at www.ICGtesting.com
Printed in the USA
BVHW040230151021
619011BV00015B/554

9 780578 913506